Collected Poems

Collected Poems

BERNARD SPENCER

✳

Edited and with an introduction by

ROGER BOWEN

Oxford New York Toronto Melbourne

OXFORD UNIVERSITY PRESS

1981

Oxford University Press, Walton Street, Oxford OX2 6DP

London Glasgow New York Toronto
Delhi Bombay Calcutta Madras Karachi
Kuala Lumpur Singapore Hong Kong Tokyo
Nairobi Dar es Salaam Cape Town
Melbourne Auckland

and associated companies in
Beirut Berlin Ibadan Mexico City

Poems © Mrs Anne Humphreys 1981
Introduction and annotation © Roger Bowen 1981

British Library Cataloguing in Publication Data

Spencer, Bernard
Collected poems.
I. Title   II. Bowen, Roger
821'.914   PR6037.P42   80–42224
ISBN 0–19–211930–3

Set by King's English Typesetters Ltd
Printed in Great Britain by
The Thetford Press Ltd, Thetford, Norfolk

CONTENTS

Contents

Contents

Contents

PREFACE

In 1965, two years after the death of Bernard Spencer, Alan Ross published the *Collected Poems*. This volume included *Aegean Islands and Other Poems* (London: Editions Poetry, 1946), and *With Luck Lasting* (London: Hodder & Stoughton, 1963), the first twenty-five poems of which had appeared in the subscriber's edition, *The Twist in the Plotting* (Reading: University of Reading School of Art, 1960). These were the three titles published during Spencer's lifetime. To this body of work Ross added 'Poems from Vienna,' a sheaf of ten, which had all appeared in *London Magazine* between September 1963 and January 1964, five posthumously. At the time of the Ross edition work in manuscript was untraced, and poems which had not been printed in volume form remained uncollected.

The present edition reprints the original published texts of *Aegean Islands*, *With Luck Lasting*, and the Vienna group from *Collected Poems*. Any exception to this rule is explained in the Notes. I have, however, followed Ross's rearrangement of sections in *Aegean Islands* by placing 'Poems before 1940' at the beginning of the volume, thereby maintaining an historical sequence. 'Poems previously uncollected and unpublished,' my fourth section, combines, in as close a chronological order as I can ascertain, all his uncollected pieces, from the first year of his publication in *New Verse*, 1935, to the last year of his contributions to *London Magazine*; and also unpublished poems dating from 1940 to 1963, of which 'Black Cat' and 'The Train Window' have recently appeared in the *London Magazine* (December 1979–January 1980). The Notes provide a full account of sources for this hitherto uncollected and unpublished material, while a bibliographical summary describes unfinished poems, fragments, and worksheets not reproduced here.

The University of Reading is the principal archive for Spencer manuscripts and papers. The core was established between 1959 and 1960, coinciding with the preparation for *The Twist in the Plotting*, and correspondence between Spencer and Ian Fletcher in connection with this volume adds usefully to the manuscript resource. In 1979 the collection was augmented with a generous gift of manuscripts, letters and notes, from the poet's widow, Mrs Anne Humphreys. The *London Magazine* collection at the Humanities Research Center, University of Texas at Austin, contains additional galleys, typescripts, and also correspondence between Spencer and John Lehmann, and Spencer and

Preface

Alan Ross. The Poetry Collection of the Lockwood Memorial Library, at the University of Buffalo (now the State University of New York at Buffalo), was the first academic library to acquire the poet's work, with a direct request made in 1950, but the items were few. The friendship between Spencer and George Seferis, which began in Greece in 1940, has insured the survival of some of Spencer's wartime poems in typescript form; these are to be found in the Seferis Papers at the Gennadius Library, American School of Classical Studies, in Athens.

Spencer's manuscript records are partial; so much, particularly from the pre-war and wartime periods, has been lost. Those public and private sources made available to me up to 1980 are acknowledged fully in the Notes.

Because of their collaborative nature, I have not included the translations from George Seferis. Spencer, Lawrence Durrell, and Nanos Valaoritis are credited as the translators for *The King of Asine and Other Poems* (London: John Lehmann, 1948), but as Durrell has explained to me (in a letter dated 16 June 1979), apart from 'Asine' which is almost entirely Durrell's version, no single poem can be identified as the work of any one translator. The volume was the result of 'committee' sessions, with Valaoritis bolstering the 'kitchen Greek' of the two English poets. Valaoritis and Spencer also collaborated in translations of Odysseus Elytis, one of which appeared in *New Writing and Daylight* 7 (1946), and another in *Penguin New Writing* 35 (1948). Translations of Rafael Alberti have apparently not survived but I have included four unpublished translations from Eugenio Montale.

To enhance an understanding of Spencer's development I have made a selection of his undergraduate poems, which were published in *Oxford Poetry*, *Oxford Outlook*, and *Sir Galahad* between 1929 and 1932. These are collected in Appendix A. Spencer was not given to disquisitions on the art of poetry, and so the rare moments when he does talk about his craft are worth saving. One prose statement, reprinted from *Personal Landscape* (1942), and one from the *Poetry Book Society Bulletin* (1963) constitute Appendix B.

I gratefully acknowledge permissions granted by the following institutions: The Library of the University of Reading; The BBC Script Library, London; The Poetry/Rare Books Collection of the University Libraries, State University of New York at Buffalo; the Humanities Research Center, University of Texas at Austin; and the Gennadius Library, American School of Classical Studies, Athens. For their kind

Preface

assistance I must thank Dr J. A. Edwards at Reading, Eric J. Carpenter at Buffalo, Ellen Dunlap at Austin, and Sophie Papageorgiou at the Gennadius. In Athens, Maro Seferis graciously allowed me access to the Seferis Papers. The British Council Staff in London, Madrid, Barcelona, Palermo, Salonika, Athens, Cairo, and Vienna have been most helpful; and I should make special mention of Jonathan Barker at the Arts Council Poetry Library.

I thank all those who have helped me with particular questions relating to the life and work, though I regret this list cannot be exhaustive: Sir Isaiah Berlin, Sir Bernard and Lady Burrows, Arthur Calder-Marshall, Dorian Cooke, Bryn Davies, Dan Davin, Lawrence Durrell, Paul Gotch, Patrick and Leslie Grier, Geoffrey Grigson, Bernard Gutteridge, David Hicks, Garnett Kempson, Francis King, John Lehmann, Robert Liddell, the late Olivia Manning, Cynthia Peppercorn, Mrs J. Spencer-Bernard, Stephen Spender, M. J. Tambimuttu, Terence Tiller, Nanos Valaoritis, and Gwyn Williams. I am grateful to John Fitzgibbon, Melanie Isaacs, and Clover Pertinez who showed me additional manuscripts. Professor Ian Fletcher, of the University of Reading, and Ruth Speirs have been primary sources of inspiration, and I owe a singular debt of gratitude to the late G. S. Fraser. Desmond Graham has helped me with certain enquiries, and his editorial and biographical work on Keith Douglas has encouraged me in my own venture. On this side of the Atlantic, my interest in Spencer has been monitored more than helpfully by Lee Van Demarr.

I am indebted above all to Mrs Anne Humphreys, who made available to me the bulk of her late husband's manuscripts and virtually all the unpublished texts; without her support and generosity this edition would not have been possible. Alan Ross's interest and help has been much appreciated. He first published my essay, 'The Edge of a Journey: Notes on Bernard Spencer' (*London Magazine,* December 1979–January 1980) – later reprinted by Dannie Abse (in slightly edited form) as 'The Anonymous Poet: Notes on Bernard Spencer' (*Best of the Poetry Year: Poetry Dimension Annual 7,* London: Robson Books, 1980) – and the Vienna portion of this introduction originates here. Finally I must thank Jacqueline Simms of Oxford University Press, who has guided me with patience and enthusiasm.

Tucson, Arizona 1980   Roger Bowen

INTRODUCTION

I

Bernard Spencer belongs squarely to the history of English poetry in the 1930s and the 1940s. A co-editor of *Oxford Poetry* with Stephen Spender, he went on to become a regular contributor to *New Verse*, to serve as assistant editor under Geoffrey Grigson, and to earn recognition as a younger member of the Auden generation. Early in the war he joined the British Council and his name was associated with a band of writers-in-exile whose home for the duration of hostilities was first Greece and then Egypt. From 1942 to 1945, in Cairo, Spencer, Lawrence Durrell, and Robin Fedden produced *Personal Landscape*, hailed by John Lehmann as 'one of the rare "little" magazines that have made literary history in our time.'[1] His first volume, *Aegean Islands and Other Poems* (1946), published by Editions Poetry London, exemplifies both his native and expatriate identities.

Outside these particular periods and associations, however, Spencer, unlike many of his contemporaries, is a strangely invisible figure. After the war, until his death in 1963, he remained a traveller and exile, though now more solitary; he displayed no obvious traits that would tie him to school or fashion. His work for the Council in Palermo, Turin, Madrid, Athens, Ankara, and Vienna, with brief periods in London, insured only a cosmopolitan badge: 'charming but always abroad,'[2] in the words of Cyril Connolly. Cut off from his pre-war and wartime literary ties, Spencer, by the very nature of his uprooted life, lost some of the connection necessary to maintain a high profile among those who kept more naturally, or more assiduously, a metropolitan address. His talent seemed out of step; he was to many the distinguished outsider. But he unobtrusively pursued his art: contemplating the domestic clutter of an Ibiza fishing boat, confronting memory and desire on an Athens street corner, and absorbing the violent presence of history on the Bosphorus. He was not a publicist for this potentially exotic marginality, and he was too concerned with a 'respect for the object' to luxuriate in bardic isolation. He did not court publishers or push himself forward; he could be unhurried and disorganized in his literary affairs, and his creative energy was frequently stalled by serious bouts of ill health. Though recognizing the charm and the wit, Stephen Spender detected, even in the undergraduate poet, a 'depressed or depressive quality'[3] which perhaps held him back from a fuller expression of his talent. In later years Spencer himself confessed to a natural 'inertia and diffidence'[4] which kept him comparatively silent for so long.

Dan Davin, who first met him in Egypt, is reminded of the inter-war heroes of Gerhardie or Waugh, characters to whom things simply happened; Spencer maintained, he said, 'an ironic acceptance of what life had to offer him. He was always waiting for the next performance.'[5] In the last year of his life it seemed that his role might well be poet *redivivus*. Hodder published *With Luck Lasting* (1963) which shared the Poetry Book Society's recommendation with Charles Tomlinson's *A Peopled Landscape*. Cyril Connolly took pleasure at a rediscovery and an evident 'new lease,' while Roy Fuller found 'substantial confirmation of renewal.'[6] Buried among Spencer's papers there is a scribbled list of reviews and anthology inclusions since 1960, the year of the subscriber's edition, *The Twist in the Plotting*. The names and titles are accompanied by a very private celebration: 'into the light at last.'[7] This, perhaps as much as we will ever find, betrays a sense of his own worth, if not the will to make an impact.

Alan Ross published an elegant collected edition in 1965. Individual poems have been randomly anthologized but, with the exception of Robin Skelton's Penguin anthologies, *Poetry of the Thirties* and *Poetry of the Forties*, editors have not been generous in their acknowledgement. Philip Larkin gives him the benefit of only one entry in the *Oxford Book of Twentieth Century English Verse* (1973). Dannie Abse made a brave effort at rehabilitation in the fifth volume of *Corgi Modern Poets in Focus* (1973), but the series was unfortunately short-lived. Aside from Abse's introduction to that selection, and an earlier essay by Martin Dodsworth, critical attention has been slight: honourable mentions for the most part by chroniclers of the 1930s and 1940s.[8] This neglect of Spencer's full history, his evolution as a poet, and the excellence and individuality of his final achievement, is regrettable. His poetry matured over some thirty-four years of sparse and irregular publication, and through a life defined by exile, journeys, by war, personal loss, and a melancholy absence of permanence: 'Even when I say I love you it is tainted with goodbyes' ('Sud-Express').

The man and his work are hard to separate. In a memorial essay by Lawrence Durrell the human and aesthetic character is acutely and sympathetically perceived: 'He had a sort of piercing, yet undogmatic irony of approach to people and things; as if he had taken up some sort of quiet vantage point inside himself from which with unerring fidelity he pronounced upon the world – not in the form of grandiose generalities, aphorisms or epigrams, but in small strict pronouncements which hit home. His best poetry is like that – a succession of plain, almost nude statements which somehow give the feeling of incontrovertibility. The feeling, the tenderness is all the purer for not being orchestrated too richly.'[9] Spencer himself is candid about a clear relationship between the life and the art. He introduced a BBC programme devoted to his own poetry with this admission: 'My poems are inclined to be autobiographical and to follow the events of my life . . . For me, poetry begins very much at home, wherever home may be.'[10] In a letter to Alan Ross written shortly before his death, he cheerfully confirms that a Vienna poem, 'On the "Sievering" Tram,' alludes to the birth of his son, and that his poems are 'always factual.'[11]

II

Charles Bernard Spencer – preparatory schoolmaster, advertising agent, film writer, BBC broadcaster, lecturer, and poet – was descended from a collateral branch of the Spencer-Churchill family. His father, Sir Charles Gordon Spencer, was a High Court Judge in Madras, where Bernard was born in 1909. Unlike Lawrence Durrell he could have no memory of Empire; he was bundled home to 'Pudding Island' as an infant. Bernard and his elder brother, John, joined their sister, Cynthia, and were brought up by relatives and guardians at first in Southampton, then in Crowell, Oxfordshire, and lastly, from the end of the Great War, in Rowner, near Gosport. Though the Solent is remembered in 'Yachts on the Nile' and 'My Sister' recreates fondly 'the fig tree in the garden' of the Rowner vicarage, Spencer's childhood seems to have been primarily an early and unbidden taste of exile and independence to which he had to accommodate himself: 'As belonging to a country clergyman's household, my brother, my sister and myself were regarded as solidly too good for the company of village children, and by the local gentry as not good by and large for the company of theirs. Consequently we made our own amusements, often separately, and this, along with any books I managed to get hold of, was probably a helpful stimulus to the imagination.'[12] At preparatory schools in Eastbourne and Stevenage Spencer nurtured that imagination and found recognition among his fellows for comic poems and adventure stories. In 1923, he followed his brother and his father to the formidably muscular world of Marlborough. Though athleticism was still very much a governing feature of

College life, Spencer could thank his housemaster, George Turner, who became Master in 1926 and was devoted to the arts, for making the aesthetes less conspicuous, if not more secure. A junior housemaster, Revd Canning, whose garden 'with its teacups and strawberries was an escape hatch to civilization,'[13] hosted the Anonymous Society for a group of boys including Spencer, Anthony Blunt, and the more senior John Betjeman and Louis MacNeice. Even in his more assured final year Spencer led an aloof, solitary life; the pursuits which most engaged this 'shy squirrel,'[14] as Betjeman recreates him, were poetry and drawing. In recollections of his early reading and appreciation, he singles out the particular impact of Masefield and Flecker and the lure of foreign settings. But there was also George Herbert: 'he has always remained one of my great admirations because of his deep feeling, his essential innocence and his sparing and curious use of words, his sense of a tight pattern.'[15] Though Spencer was to discover for himself Flecker's 'white Aegean isles among the foam,' this adherence to a sense of pattern, this spareness, is what distinguishes his Mediterranean poems, those for which he is perhaps best known. The curiosity here is not the foreign or the exotic so much as the patterning of language which must convey with precision the colour and excitement, or the melancholy and estrangement. This emphasis on the act and language of perception invariably directs our attention inward; the external discovery is only the beginning.

At Marlborough Spencer was a quietly successful artist, and this early talent is certainly reflected in the poetry, with its painterly eye and habit, its pictorial exactness. The much anthologized 'Part of Plenty,' for example, has the careful detailing of a still life, while 'The Boats' begins: 'Five boats beside the lake,/pulled bow first up the shore; how hard it is/to draw them, from each angle changing, elegant.' The village craftsman in 'On a Carved Axle-Piece from a Sicilian Cart' is admired for his art, as is the sculptor in 'Sarcophagi.' In 'The Ship' the 'simple beach and sea' are 'like elementary shapes a child has drawn.' 'Fluted Armour' describes the 'world-gaze of the great Italians' in the National Gallery and the restoration of the jaded poet to a sense of 'particular things.' Of his own painting and drawing after Marlborough and Oxford we have no account; it is a hobby that seems to have been abandoned, but it continues to thrive in his poems.

The Oxford of Michaelmas, 1928, had lost its famous generation of aesthetes, though *The Cherwell* that year was still celebrating their London lives; the dandies of the late twenties could not match that notoriety. Spencer, a Gentleman Commoner at Corpus Christi, in his soft tweeds, bow tie and sidewhiskers, certainly affected a bohemian lifestyle. In his first term his room was raided at dawn by a predictable band of hearties who removed one of those sidewhiskers. Undaunted, Spencer refused to shave off the other, continued to read *transition*, and to decorate his lampshade with 'surrealist, mildly obscene figures in pencil,'[16] as his closest friend at Corpus, Isaiah Berlin, vividly remembers.

In *World Within World* Stephen Spender, after the departure of Auden, recalls adopting a 'new circle of contemporaries who had interests in common: MacNeice, Spencer, Arthur Calder-Marshall, and Humphrey House.'[17] There was a distinct Oxford brotherhood, *just* post-Auden, and Spencer certainly played his part in the university's literary world from 1929 to 1932. He contributed poems and art criticism to *Sir Galahad*, edited by MacNeice, and poems, reviews and art features to *Oxford Outlook*, edited at different times by Calder-Marshall and Berlin. Most significant of all was his participation in the Blackwell annual, *Oxford Poetry*. One poem, 'Festa,' appeared in the 1929 volume, compiled by Spender and MacNeice; Spencer went on to become editor with Spender in 1930, and with Richard Goodman in 1931. The 1932 issue, dedicated with reverence to 'Wystan Auden, Cecil Day Lewis, and Stephen Spender,' continued to include his work. His reviews and art criticism, though informed and energetic, suffered from overstatement. His own creative impulses as a poet, rather than the critical sorties he later felt he had no true instinct for, show a very different sensibility at work: circumspect, sensitive, and puzzled rather than overwhelmed by the sharp mysteries of love and Nature. In early poems like 'Schedules' and 'Festa' there are some of the telling visual touches we associate with the mature poet, but at this stage he seems particularly governed by an insatiable, cumulative style derived from Auden and MacNeice. His characteristic Oxford voice, however, is contemplative; the poems are frequently dialogues with self, tightly wound, obstinately private, with a nod here to Hopkins, here to Eliot. But what they all show is a seriousness of purpose, a craftmanship, and a suspicion of conventional image and sentiment. At his best, for instance, in 'For seeing whole I had been too near my friends,' we can perceive a broadening of his lyric expertise and recognize that subtle accessibility which was to define his later work.

III

In 1932 Spencer left Oxford with a second-class degree in Greats and disappeared into London life, 'an exceptionally sensitive and intelligent man and a genuinely gifted writer,'[18] as Berlin assesses his under-graduate companion. But he had never been fully engaged with his university studies, nor committed to any future beyond Oxford, and, compared with his contemporaries, he was very reticent about his identity as a poet. From 1932 to 1940 he earned a precarious living as a preparatory schoolmaster in a variety of positions; he worked as a copy-writer in an advertising agency, and as a script-writer for a film company; he co-wrote an earnest biography of a Victorian civil servant, Sir Henry Cunynghame, for Michael Joseph,[19] and in 1936, in Hampstead, he married Nora Gibbs, a tall, striking actress with an uncertain career in provincial repertory. None of these accomplish-ments was becoming for the second son of a judge in the Indian Civil Service, and the absence of a volume of verse in these pre-war years did not befit a junior member of the Auden generation. Writing to John Lehmann in the summer of 1938 he did declare that he 'had enough poems for a book' and that Geoffrey Grigson had recommended he try Lehmann's publishing house, but nothing was to come of this inquiry. His participation in the 'collective text' of the decade is confirmed in other ways: his association with *New Verse* from 1935 to 1938 and his substantial representation in *New Verse: An Anthology* (1939); random appearances in *The Spectator* and *The Listener*, and a place won in *The Century's Poetry*, vol. 2, 'Bridges to the Present Day.' The poems are modest in quantity, to be sure, but authentic and vigorous.

The 'mild, left-wing sympathies'[20] attributed to him in the 1930s can take on a more assertive tone in the formulaic 'Evasions' and can harden into a declaration of faith, at the conclusion of 'Waiting': 'If we live we have the pride/To be capable of action, to speak out plainly. The wise and passionate/Are on our side.' But in poems like 'A Cold Night' and 'A Thousand Killed', which are generated by the suffering of the Spanish Civil War, there is a response to the pressures of conscience rather than the events themselves, and a recognition of the limits of ideology. The authority of heart and hearth is particularly strong in 'A Cold Night,' where the poet strives to maintain his own integrity in the face of 'this season, this century.' A quietist impulse is present, too, in the pastoral silence which concludes 'Going to the Country,' but it is in 'Allotments: April,' his most anthologized, and most achieved pre-war poem, that his desire for more private solutions, for a separate peace, become clear. The 'wireless voice repeating pacts, persecutions,/And imprisonments and deaths and heaped violent deaths,' and the 'sour doorways of the poor,' claim their inevitable portion of an April day in 1936, but a more localised curiosity attends to 'the big veins/Sprawled over the beet-leaf, light-red fires/Of flower pots heaped by the huts,' and Spencer finds solace ultimately in a Yeatsian image of 'two elms and their balanced attitude like dancers, their arms like dancers.' In a miniature manifesto written for *Personal Landscape* in 1942 (see Appendix B) he finds suspect the 'capacity for pity' and the 'capacity for scientific detatchment' when used as governing principles in poetry. The poet should not seek these 'attitudes of separation' but 'attitudes of joining': 'True poetry is a dance in which you take part and enjoy yourself.'[21] His discomfort with so much of the programme of his generation's poetry, his own sense of what he was later to call the 'strangling influence of what was considered right in those days,'[22] is clearly displayed here only two years after his discovery of Greece, a culture and above all a landscape which offered him the artistic solution he was looking for. Expatriation and the happy collisions with non-Anglo-Saxon cultures gave Spencer, a most reluctant ideologue, a welcome alternative to that 'collective text.' He was able to escape what Spender later referred to as the 'time-bound'[23] generation and to experience the affirmation of being 'picked clean from the world,' and being master of poems not dependent on fashion or movement.

IV

In 1940, after eight years of uncertainty, Spencer left England for a Council posting in Salonika, and, except for short intervals, he was to live abroad thereafter. This new life began in a cold February, on the main line from Belgrade to Athens: 'As I passed the wild and rocky gorges of southern Yugoslavia and entered Greece, the sun came out and there was no more snow. This gave me the forcible impression of leaving the Europe I knew and entering a strange country.' This simple travel note, from a BBC talk given in 1946,[24] lends an allegorical touch to Spencer's journey, but the paradise beyond the mountains was being threatened; within eight months the Graeco-Italian War had broken out. His wife returned to London before the fall of France and by Christmas, 1940, Spencer found himself kicking his heels in Athens, waiting for a Council transfer to Fuad I University in Cairo, which eventually took place early in the new year. The evacuation of Athens was completed by May 1941, and Salonika had already been abandoned in March. Greece, for Spencer, was barely a year, but it was enough.

Salonika was 'a very Macedonian town, rather primitive, smelling strongly of fish and fruit and the kind of resinous wood which is burned everywhere as fuel . . . The town with its bay is set among wild, barren hills, and in winter . . . it is intensely cold, especially when a north-east wind, the Varda, sweeps down from Russia.'[25] The city, a centre of operations for the Albanian campaign, is the setting for his first war poems. The air-raids began on the last day of October 1940; Spencer's room at the Hotel Luxembourg was demolished and he was billeted with other staff members. The British Institute was damaged in several bombardments and closed by the police; an Italian bomber plunged burning into Aristotle Square, to the seaward side of the Institute, its shrivelled pilot trapped in the wreckage for the curious to see. 'Salonika June 1940,' 'Base Town,' and 'Death of an Airman' record successive stages of Spencer's encounter with his first foreign home and the war which overwhelmed it.

But there was another Greece he discovered between his winter arrival in Macedonia and his departure from its battered capital: he spent the month of August, his first leave, on the island of Mykonos, where he joined forces with the young Greek poet, Nanos Valaoritis, and Lawrence Durrell, then a Council field man in Kalamata. Here, in the Cyclades, Spencer had more leisure to absorb the colour and texture of land and seascape, and ponder the history which is never far from the eye. In 'Peasant Festival,' which dates from this summer idyll, his deeper interest in 'people in a landscape, with some dramatic situation,' and the conjunction of landscape and feeling, is made vivid; and in 'Delos' the drama is recovered from a mercantile as well as a mythic past. 'Aegean Islands 1940–41' was written during his Cairo exile and of all his Greek poems it most perfectly captures his liberating introduction to a geography, astonishing and immediate, which embodied a rich sense of the past.

> To sun one's bones beside the
> Explosive, crushed-blue, nostril-opening sea
> (The weaving sea, splintered with sails and foam,
> Familiar of famous and deserted harbours,
> Of coins with dolphins on and fallen pillars.)

Introduction

The poem is built, appropriately, on infinitive constructions, and it celebrates with its supple rhythms an infinitude of personal memories and cultural sympathies, all secured with an exactness of detail, from the 'ribbed, lionish coast' to the 'dark bread/The island wine.' The movement of the lyric is headlong, ever expanding, but the rational, meditative voice which speaks with the knowledge of loss, allows the poem to reach its main clause and call to order these 'elements of a happiness.' As Durrell remarks of Spencer, 'Greece woke him up'. Both writers on leaving Greece were to suffer from what Durrell describes in 'Epilogue in Alexandria' (*Prospero's Cell*) as the pain of 'amputation'.

Home was now Egypt: 'English exiles. England's reply to Goebbels. The British Council's legion. There's a colony of them here driven from the Balkans. Nice chaps, some of them.' This is the minimally charitable description of Spencer's Cairo given by Braun, in Dan Davin's *For the Rest of Our Lives* (1947), an account of the desert campaign and the crossed paths of civilian and military in Alexandria and Cairo. Olivia Manning's *The Levant Trilogy* (1977–1980) alludes, if obliquely, to some of the same personalities. It was a unique accident of literary history; Terence Tiller and Robin Fedden were already on the English Faculty at the university, teaching in a department which had originally been set up by Robert Graves in 1926. Spencer was seconded here in January 1941, arriving in Cairo with Robert Liddell, while a flood of refugees came from Athens in May. There was Olivia Manning, married to one of the 'legion', R. D. Smith; and John Speirs, another Council lecturer, whose Latvian wife, Ruth, was to publish a volume of Rilke translations in Cairo and contribute to *Personal Landscape*. She was a close friend of Spencer and an invaluable critic of his work both during and after the war. Some of his later poems, notably 'Sud-Express,' are addressed to her. Durrell spent some time in Cairo, sharing a flat with Spencer, but was destined for information work in Alexandria, where he kept literary company with Liddell and Harold Edwards, the Skelton scholar, both of whom assisted Gwyn Williams in the English Department at the University of Alexandria. There was George Seferis, who had been evacuated from Crete and was to represent his exiled government in Pretoria before returning to Cairo as Press Officer in 1942; and Elie Papadimitriou, who also wrote for *Personal Landscape* and was to move later to Palestine. On leave from the Western Desert, sharing companionship and poetry, with Spencer in particular, was Keith Douglas.

Introduction

From Davin's novel, the poet Peter Anderson, a composite figure, as
is Castlebar in the Manning books, complains of the cultural isolation:
'It's not much good for a poet. Too cut off.' A uniformed companion
responds: 'Still, Cairo is an intellectual capital for the time being. You
might as well make the best of it.' They did, and *Personal Landscape* is a
testament to the discrimination of its editors. Spencer wrote, too, for
Citadel, the Council's journal, *Esfam*, the English Faculty publication, reviewed for the *Egyptian Mail*, lectured the troops on Greece
and Art History and, on a less formal basis, engaged in a private verse
war, a 'flyting,' between Cairo and Alexandria. One salvo from him is
worth recording: 'But oh what startled muse would not miscarry/when
in the swollen verse of Durrell (Larry)/pornography and Greece and
gaga marry.'[26]

A sybaritic life in the Egyptian capital was perhaps encouraged – beer
and billiards at the Anglo-Egyptian Union on Gezira Island, sipping
coffee in the garden of Groppi's Café, even the distractions of Mère
Rolland's establishment – but there was rarely the means to support
such a life to its full. Spencer shared crowded flats in central Cairo,
coped with bed bugs, the discomfort of the khamseen, observed the
egregious poverty about him, the 'flap' before Alamein, and prepared at
that time for a refugee flight to Palestine. As Robin Fedden points out it
was the 'length and inconvenience' of the struggle that they endured
rather than any inspiration or danger; it was a period of 'stagnation,' of
'bone mould, temples, temporal and cultural isolation, an unreal
society and a long war.'[27] Ian Fletcher, serving with the army in Egypt,
finds in the expatriate voice of Spencer's Egyptian poems something
akin to 'disembodiment . . . an unreality not purely physical but
extending to motives and relations.'[28] In 'Letter Home', a Cairo poem
not published until 1960, the poet walks a petal-strewn street in
Zamalek looking for a house number: 'City where I live, not home,
road that flowers with police,/what in all worlds am I doing here?' The
descriptive exuberance which characterized his Greek phase may be
seen again in, say, the alliterative transformations which begin 'Egyptian Delta,' but here, too, is a marked sense of alienation. He is drawn
repeatedly to the sombre image of the ox with his bound eyes patiently
going his round, and the scene before him is an enticement to lose
track, to be 'no longer a person or sad,' to separate himself from an
identity which is both painful and unreal. The setting in 'Yachts on the
Nile' has a fragile hold; he finds instead an uneasy solace in memories
of other times, places, and people, and is only persuaded that 'we are

born with some nostalgia/to make the migration of sails/and wings a crying matter.'

V

During the last year of the war, his wife was able to join him for the short interval before a return to London and a nearly twelve-month wait for membership of the permanent overseas service of the Council. London, from 1945 to 1946, and on later occasions between appointments or on extended leave, was a time for casual reunions and for waiting, for a modicum of work in talks and overseas educational programming for the BBC, and in the immediate post-war interlude Tambimuttu's Fitzrovia provided a social and a literary anchor. Ill health, however, dogged both Bernard and Nora, and Spencer's professional advancement was delayed; a position at the University of Rome, working with Mario Praz, was recommended but had to be passed over.

His first peacetime appointment proved to be a less than ideal reintroduction to Europe; in September, 1946, the Spencers arrived in Palermo. 'The set-up is bandits, black market, maleesh, street cries, general confusion, heat, dust, cold flooding rain, a beautiful island and a rather shabby little town.'[29] Ironically, this move, and the months that followed, coincided with an unusual spurt of energy and a growing public identity. Late in 1946 his belated first volume, *Aegean Islands and Other Poems*, appeared, and was acquired by Doubleday for an American edition; during the new year a collaborative translation of Seferis, *The King of Asine and Other Poems*, with Nanos Valaoritis and Durrell, was being prepared for John Lehmann. In addition, Lehmann found a place for him, as an original contributor and translator, in *Penguin New Writing*. The Spencer whom Durrell remembers in Cairo, quietly scolding his co-editors for their phrase-making and wild ambition, and confessing to be 'never one for the long haul,'[30] was actually planning 'to get most of another book of poems finished [that] year.'[31]

This was not to be. A tubercular condition, for which Nora had been treated in London before their departure for Sicily, returned. There were urgent calls for a transfer, and in the Spring term of 1947 they travelled to Rome for more expert treatment and a more agreeable climate. But these measures came too late; in June she died from heart failure caused by the tuberculosis, and was buried in the Protestant

Cemetery. 'At Courmayeur,' published two years later, is an elegy on the loss of Nora, who was to have accompanied Bernard that summer on an Alpine holiday in the Valle d'Aosta; it is an address to a companion who 'for ever stayed behind,' and a recognition of a life which can so haphazardly resist our plans: 'Guesses went wide.' Misfortune was to prevail: now serving in Turin, in an equally unsuitable climate, Spencer himself was stricken with tuberculosis and moved to a clinic in Leysin, Switzerland where he underwent a painful cure. 'In a Foreign Hospital' records that time and his confrontation 'with our bit of death inside us/(nearer than that Death our whole life lies under).' He returned to England in December, 1948, and was considered fit only for 'light duties' at the Council's Davies Street headquarters until the autumn of 1949 when he was posted to Madrid.

Spencer's career from this point forward is anchored in the Spanish capital; his first period of residence ended in the summer of 1955, and he returned there in September, 1958 for another four years. Between the first and second Spanish sojourns lie the odd and melancholy parentheses of Athens and Ankara, a reacquaintance with the eastern Mediterranean which fell short of expectation. While in Cairo, Greece's 'stony islands' had inspired a more acute nostalgia than his 'grassy home'; he experienced the comradeship of Greek and British exiles in Egypt during the war, and in 'A Spring Wind,' written in 1946, he is moved by the Aegean echoes of Elytis's verse, and by the image of 'haunted Seferis, smiling, playing with beads.' At the time of Spencer's transfer to Athens in September, 1955 the Cyprus crisis was refusing to leave this ideal past intact. Shortly before his arrival, the old Institute on Ermou Street was bombed and the new headquarters on Kolonaki Square had a resident detective and police guards. Though critical of British policies, Spencer was undoubtedly wounded by the volte-face in Anglo-Greek relations, as the despairing incredulity of 'The Rendez-vous' suggests. The youthful philhellenism of wartime, the yearning in 'A Spring Wind' for 'Athens,/her blinded marble heads,/her pepper trees, the bare heels of her girls,' are blunted now by the 'cry of crowds and doors slammed to.'

Ankara was not without its political tensions; a pencil bomb destroyed an armchair he had recently vacated in a hotel lounge, and the University of Ankara, where he lectured, was the scene of frequent agitation. He was there six months, from January to July, 1958, and, apart from 'The Beginning,' with its Bosphorus setting, only one other poem, 'Delicate Grasses,' and a short, unpublished journal, 'Road to

Kanya,' describing a car journey across the Anatolian Plain to the Gulf of Antalya, provide a record of this eastern venture.

The resumption of Madrid life certainly confirmed an urban bias in Spencer's poetry: the cafés, bars, the lottery-sellers on the street corners, the suburban apartment blocks, the bullfight, the circus, the sounds, and the human isolation. Though he travelled within Spain and to the Balearics, there is now comparatively little inspiration derived from landscape. The expansiveness of 'Boat Poem' stands out, as does the affectionate inventiveness of 'Cripples,' but he makes no confident attempt to 'capture' Spain as he had Greece. With the ghostly presence of 'Roman vanguards' in 'Near Aranjuez' there is a momentary, unforced return to historical perspective, but in 'Castille,' an unpublished poem, we can see an unusually self-conscious attempt to embrace the culture that surrounds him, in its 'boulder and scrub and mountains shaped like pain;/hearts that ferment with gold and dust, dead bones and crowns and flowers.' Spencer's world now shows far less of this panoramic effect; it is smaller, more private.

VI

There is, in the years that followed the death of Nora, a discernible sense of retreat in the life and the poetry, a consolidation of an innate reticence and a preference for anonymity. To begin with, his Council career afforded him a haven from undue responsibility. Wherever his posting, he earned a reputation as a much-loved and effective teacher; indeed, his unobtrusive elegance and urbanity marked him off as a Council officer of the old school, but his administrative abilities were minimal, and his energies did not extend far beyond the classroom and certain social duties. He kept his head low, was not ambitious for advancement, and his employer, accordingly, made few demands. But his spare hours continued to be filled with the company of friends, café conversation, and the amusements of city life. Occasional periodical publication signals the writer still at work, but his life to a degree seems governed by a fear of the solitude a full commitment to his art would demand. Contemplating the wild beauty which surrounds a ruined Greek theatre, in 'Delicate Grasses,' he is compelled to recognize an even more powerful impulse:

> There is no name for such strong liberation;
> I drift their way: I need what their world lends;

then, chilled by one thought further still than those,
I swerve towards life and friends
before the trap fangs close.

The 'strong liberation' from which he turns here would require a willingness to surrender to what an attentive reviewer of Spencer's contribution to *New Verse: An Anthology* had termed, the 'right overtones of ecstacy.'[32] He probably had in mind the unifying vision which closes 'Allotments: April' and secures the poet's participation in the 'dance.' This 'ecstacy,' indeed, is most frequently achieved in Spencer's stirring final phrases. In his post-war work one thinks of 'On a Carved Axle-Piece,' 'A Spring Wind,' 'Cripples,' 'Castanets,' and the 'traffic/gongs ringing like glory' which bring 'On the "Sievering" Tram' to its close. Increasingly, however, after *Aegean Islands*, there is a pull away from the ecstatic towards the elegiac, and, at its most extreme, an enclosing sense of alienation.

'At Courmayeur' and 'In a Foreign Hospital,' which stand together in *With Luck Lasting*, suggest an emotional watershed in his life and his work. The first, as I have already noted, is dedicated to his wife, while the second contends with his own brush with death. A sense of radical separation distinguishes both poems, and it is in the Leysin clinic that he acknowledges by way of compensation for 'dearer names' and 'easier beds,' elsewhere and out of reach, a freedom to 'keep . . . watch with images.' The images present on this occasion – the 'bare, white room, the World, an insect's rage' – though suggesting a claustrophobic futility, still bear out that freedom of perception, still harbour a possibility: 'And if I am lucky, find some link, some link.' In 'Pino', an uncollected poem from the same period, life is defined as 'a time of waiting . . ./ But waiting sometimes vivid with the sign/of things amazingly connected.' Spencer maintains his watch, waits for those moments of connection, and frequently must report that there has been no link. But he persists in picking out, with magnificent attentiveness, the world's inscape, moved not by faith but by a kind of fastidious astonishment. He takes, as Martin Dodsworth has remarked, a Rousseauistic view, of phenomena unrefined by intelligence and unmoved by the poet's presence.[33] The relationship between the observer and the phenomenal world can be governed by a respect for safe distance – the mountain peaks in 'The Train Window,' wearing 'the authority of/all-there-is-to-be-said-about-a-problem' – and can sometimes be fraught with anxiety, as in 'Witness,' where a tape-recorder and a camera, with 'thing-born' talents, threaten the poet with their own, animistic 'respect for the object.' More typically there is a melancholy recognition of the different separations which make up the 'communal' experience of the city. In 'From my Window', the students playing bowls, the rich apartment dwellers, 'their meaningless finny gestures, dumb departures and entries;/a deaf man's theatre twenty times,' the 'children of the poor,' the watchdog who lifts his head 'at a barking that chips a hole in distance', and the recording poet, are all divided from one another. The 'tall and scarecrow' musician, in 'Mediterranean Suburbs', invades the 'streets of flats, new and forbidding', and turns the corner 'like the grotesque of some need/we had forgotten that we were starving from,/or promise we have broken.' The stranger, with the 'stammering music' of his pipe does not belong to this world of 'houses for next year, evening, restless houses,' and to the poet this odd figure *ought* to be significant, ought, perhaps to promise salvation, but connections falter in the end; the darkened sky can only offer a 'wild guess' as the pipe player disappears. As in the haunting and disturbing, 'By a Breakwater,' we are left with the fragility of 'almost recognition.'

There is an urge towards silence in these post-war poems, towards an art of the minimal; keeping watch with images, he ties his poems to objects, sometimes to sensuous, sometimes to sombre particulars. At the same time, his role as exile lends itself more and more to metaphysical definition; he discusses 'Notes by a Foreigner' in these terms, when he declares that 'the poem is not just about Madrid but about any town, and eventually it is about the strangeness of being in the world at all, the feeling that you may have invented the whole thing.'[34] The evidence of retreat, however, goes far beyond the withdrawal to lowered expectations that we associate with the Movement poets. Spencer stands back from the world, sometimes silenced by a failure of connection, but never crippled by the full potential of irony. He remains doggedly curious, and, if he has to identify himself as a stranger, he is, as Dannie Abse has said, impressively 'wideawake.'[35]

Spencer paid scant attention to publication in the 1950s; that we hear from him at all has a lot to do with the persistence of those who had recognized the strength and originality of his first volume. It was in 1955 that John Lehmann first published his work in *London Magazine*; Alan Ross (who had reviewed *Aegean Islands* in *Tribune*) took over the editorship from Lehmann in April, 1961, and so the journal had become Spencer's primary, if not sole link with a reading public. Ian Fletcher invited to him to pull together ten or more years of writing for

The Twist in the Plotting, privately printed by the University of Reading School of Art in 1960. This slender edition of only twenty-five poems achieved little visibility but it did receive a better-than-grudging nod from Alvarez's poetry column in *The Observer*, a magnum of champagne from *London Magazine*, and praise from Ross for the author: 'this most sparing, personal, and compassionate of contemporary poets.'[36]

VII

There was by this time another restorative influence at work. On 29 September, 1961, Spencer was married to Anne Marjoribanks in Madrid, where they had met some three years before. A transfer to Vienna followed in the autumn of 1962, his first central European appointment and a sharp break from the Mediterranean landscapes and cities he had known for so long. But with Anne, and the son born to them that winter, he was rediscovering a 'part of plenty,' and engaging more positively with his art. Before departing for Vienna he had contracted with Hodder and Stoughton for *With Luck Lasting*, and was 'delighted to be taken on by the publishers of Bulldog Drummond.'[37] He had also recorded a reading of his poems and the Orr interview for the Council and the Ford Foundation. His wife testifies to a new drive 'to get everything out' during that Austrian year. In a letter to Ross, Spencer confesses: 'I am writing a good deal more now so I have been in the novel position, for me, of being able to make a selection.'[38]

In Vienna he was forced to accommodate a strikingly new sense of place, 'living on the edge of millions of miles of central Europe and Russia and cold and fur hats and emptiness.' The city's street life he described as 'very correct and solemn,' burrowing instead underground where the weinkellers, 'great warrens of black oak tables and timbers,' compensated for the gravity of temperament and climate in this 'Dumpling Town.'[39]

Their move to Vienna coincided with Austria's worst winter since 1841: 'It hangs over our lives like some appalling curse. The snow never goes, and people stagger through the streets with faces twisted by the cold . . . You hardly ever see the sun, and there is a cold wind characteristic of Vienna which scratches your face like the claws of a cat.' 'Poems from Vienna,' a sheaf added to the collected edition of 1965, depicts this winter-haunted city, while the last poem in the group, 'Traffic in April,' celebrates zestfully a release from hibernation.

Spain is undoubtedly missed – separation is a strong element in 'Clemente,' – but Vienna, a unique setting in his long experience of living abroad, had begun to make a special impression on the poet's art.

Towards the end of August, 1963, Bernard, Anne and the infant Piers left for an Adriatic beach resort near Venice, but this summer break was cut short by an illness which had begun to show itself earlier that year. The primary symptom was fatigue and oversleeping, and in the later stages there were blackouts and short periods of memory loss. X-rays and blood tests revealed nothing. Upon their return to Vienna his physician recommended a series of residential examinations at a private clinic. On the morning of 10 September with a fever of 102 and unable at times to identify familiar people and surroundings, he was admitted. By the time his doctor had arrived in the early afternoon he had disappeared; no one had seen him leave.

At 5 o'clock the following morning, the driver of a local Vienna-Huetteldorf train saw a body lying beside the track about eight kilometres out of the West Station. Spencer was dead from a fractured skull; he had either wandered on to the line and been struck by a train or had boarded a train at the terminus, fallen from a door, and been struck by a locomotive travelling in the opposite direction. No physical cause of the progressive neurological collapse which preceded this tragic death was ever formally identified, and those last hours and the exact circumstances of his death can never be plotted. He was cremated in Vienna and his ashes were returned to England; they lie at his parents' grave in the tiny churchyard of Wheatfield, Oxfordshire.

VIII

At fifty-three Spencer still had something of the faun about him; the loping, yet oddly stylish gait, the subtle good looks, the lop-sided smile. G. S. Fraser's memorial poem captures the witty, casual poet-expatriate in the guise most of his English friends recognized: 'Once a year,/Home from Madrid,/Istanbul, Athens,/Come to feed/Pals whom the smoke/of London hazed/With the southern *clarté*/His poems phrased//Poised on a quick,/Delicate, mocking/Poet's voice.'[40] Looking back on a shared Cairo exile George Seferis remembers 'his slim outline appearing for the aperitif we would drink at Groppi's Cafe,'[41] and a recent manuscript pushed shyly across the table between them. Geoffrey Grigson summons up the visitor to his Hampstead home before the war: 'Bernard was a sprite, of rather low pressure; you looked and he wasn't there, and then a shape came back, and he was palpable again, gentle and sweet in temper.'[42]

Spencer, elusive and palpable, is readily spirited forth from the memories of those who knew him, yet the 'permanent and individual mark [left] . . . on English poetry since the 1930s'[43] remains largely unexamined and unappreciated. Overshadowed by the more publicly active members of the Auden school in the pre-war years and, as a post-war exile, by the robust figure of Lawrence Durrell, Spencer lived in the margins of literary reputation, an unassuming and, at times, almost anonymous figure, inevitably defined by his slender output. Robin Fedden suggests a sound reason for the comparatively few poems Spencer produced, and returns us to the poet's assertions about his relationship with his art: 'Everything he wrote arose directly from personal experience . . . He never "made" poems; he only wrote when he had something to say that called imperatively for expression. It is perhaps for this reason that his work, as is rarely the case with contemporary poets, presents a mirror image of the man.'[44]

When Spencer finds himself, as he describes it, 'in a situation, out of which comes a so-far unformulated excitement,' when he recognizes the 'signal'[45] and is compelled to answer the call of the poem, the experience and the voice are uniquely his. Elements of the modern tradition may be discerned but they are well assimilated and subservient to his own instincts. If he heeded Auden's dictum – 'Report well; begin with objects and events' – he already owed much to Hardy's eye for the world's particulars, his sense of the boundaries of that world, *and* the desire for, if sometimes the fear of, moments of transcendence. A quiet precision of tone, a scrupulous and often magical power of observation, also recall Edward Thomas and Robert Frost.

Though Spencer claims no direct influence, it is clear that his emancipation from some of the conventions of the 1930s poetic, his awakening to other modes of writing, stems in good part from his exposure to contemporary Greek poetry. Seferis, especially, served to inspire. In Spencer's infrequent commentaries on his art and its 'bare bones/of motive' the name of his friend recurs: 'I learnt long ago from the Greek poet, George Seferis, to think of poems as sometimes waiting around to be written, perhaps in certain parts of a town, until a poet comes along.'[46] Seferis had contributed to the series, 'Ideas about Poetry,' for *Personal Landscape*, and on that occasion had stressed: 'All poems written or unwritten exist. I don't mean a Platonic but a biological existence. Their relation to their written form is the relation of the model to its portrait. The special ability of the poet is to see them . . .'[47] In sum, Seferis taught Spencer to wait, to trust in discovery, and not to fabricate.

A characteristic poem by Bernard Spencer lies at the intersection of place, situation, and a controlling sensibility that implies rather than declares its presence. And not the least of the poet's merits is the way in which the "written" poem somehow alerts us, to all the 'unrecognized poems which are lived through every moment of [one's] life.'[48] In 'Blue Arm,' for instance, "a problem of writing' is resolved by the discovery of the poem waiting outside his window, a poem ordinary yet extra-ordinary, composed of 'a high pink wall; plaster in map shapes peeling;/ socks on the dangle,' and the dream-like blur of sound and light in the courtyard below. There is the moment of recognition and the poem comes into being:

> Above the laughing
> animation the blue arm pushes a window; sunstabs
> are shaken my way over tree-tops. Heliographing.

NOTES TO INTRODUCTION

1. John Lehmann, *In My Own Time: Memoirs of a Literary Life* (Boston: Little, Brown, 1969), p. 339.

2. Cyril Connolly, review of *With Luck Lasting, Sunday Times*, July 14, 1963, p. 24.

3. In a letter to the editor, dated Dec. 4, 1979.

4. Letter to Alan Ross, Nov. 12. 1961, from Madrid; from the London Magazine Collection, Humanities Research Center, University of Texas at Austin. Hereafter cited as (HRC).

5. In an interview with the editor, Oxford, Nov. 16, 1978.

6. Connolly, loc. cit.; Roy Fuller, *London Magazine*, July 1963, p. 91.

7. Private papers, in the possession of Mrs Anne Humphreys. This source hereafter cited as (AH).

8. Martin Dodsworth's review-essay, 'Bernard Spencer,' is reprinted in *The Modern Poet: Essays from the Review* (London: Macdonald, 1968), pp. 90–100; consult also Roger Bowen, 'Native and Exile: The Poetry of Bernard Spencer,' *Malahat Review* (January, 1979), pp. 5–27. Further references may be found in the following texts: John Press, *A Map of Modern English Verse* (London: Oxford University Press, 1969), pp. 199, 202, 232; A. T. Tolley, *The Poetry of the Thirties* (London: Gollancz, 1975), pp. 214–17; A. Kingsley Weatherhead, *Stephen Spender and the Thirties* (Lewisburg: Bucknell U. P., 1975), pp. 88–89, 114–15; Samuel Hynes, *The Auden Generation: Literature and Politics in the Thirties* (London: Bodley Head, 1976), pp. 298–99; Robert Hewison, *Under Siege: Literary Life in London 1939–45* (London: Weidenfeld & Nicolson, 1977), pp. 121–22; Bernard Bergonzi, *Reading the Thirties* (London: Macmillan, 1978), pp. 60, 98. Covering a wider field, David Holbrook alludes to the neglected strengths of Spencer's work in *Lost Bearings in English Poetry* (London: Vision Press, 1977), pp. 173, 206. A tribute from an admirer at the University of Madrid, Professor Estéban Pujals, may be found in 'La Inspiracion Mediterranea de Bernard Spencer', *Drama, Pensiamento Y Poesia En La Literatura Inglesa* (Madrid: Ediciones Rialp, 1965), pp. 433–47.

9. Lawrence Durrell, 'Bernard Spencer,' *London Magazine*, Jan. 1964, pp. 42–43.

10. 'Poems by Bernard Spencer,' pre-recorded July 30, 1959, Third Programme (BBC Script Library).

11. June 14, 1963, from Vienna (HRC).

12. Notes for a public lecture, delivered at the University of Madrid in March, 1962 (AH).

13. From an unpublished memoir attributed to C.R.J. [Cyril Ramsay Jones], a fellow Marlburian (AH).

14. John Betjeman, 'Louis MacNeice and Bernard Spencer,' *London Magazine*, December 1963, p. 63.

15. University of Madrid lecture (AH).

16. In a letter to the editor, dated March 20, 1980.

17. Stephen Spender, *World Within World* (London: Hamish Hamilton, 1951), p. 70.

18. In an interview with the editor, London, January 10, 1979.

19. With C. H. Dudley-Ward; the book was published in 1938.

20. Kenneth Allott, ed., *Penguin Book of Contemporary Verse* (1950; rpt. Harmondsworth, Middlesex: Penguin Books, 1962), p. 229.

xxxii

21. 'Ideas About Poems III,' *Personal Landscape*, 1, pt. 4 (1942; rpt. Nendeln, Liechtenstein: Kraus, 1969), p. 2.

22. 'Bernard Spencer,' *The Poet Speaks*, ed. Peter Orr (London: Routledge & Kegan Paul, 1966), p. 234.

23. *World Within World*, p. 287.

24. Reprinted in *The Listener*, July 25 1946, pp. 108–9.

25. Spencer, Madrid University lecture (AH).

26. Manuscript in the possession of Gwyn Williams; this extract is reproduced with his kind permission.
    It should be remarked that in all this literary bustle there was a rival magazine, *Salamander*, edited by Keith Bullen, and there were a number of writers resident in Cairo – Freya Stark, Albert Cossery, P. H. Newby – who escaped these editorial nets. The Salamander Society produced the Middle East servicemen's verse anthology *Oasis* in 1943, and the Salamander Oasis Trust has reprinted this volume, with the addition of new material. *Return to Oasis* (London: Shepheard-Walwyn/Editions Poetry London, 1980) is introduced by the civilian, Lawrence Durrell.

27. Robin Fedden, 'An Anatomy of Exile,' *Personal Landscape: An Anthology of Exile* (London: Editions Poetry, 1945), p. 12.

28. Ian Fletcher, 'New Verse,' Dec. 12, 1954, Third Programme (BBC Script Library).

29. In a letter to David Hicks, dated January 25, 1947.

30. *London Magazine*, Jan. 1964, p. 44.

31. Letter to Hicks, dated May 24, 1947.

32. *The Listener*, Sept. 21, 1939, p. 589.

33. *The Modern Poet: Essays from the Review*, p. 97.

34. Madrid lecture (AH).

35. Dannie Abse, ed., *Corgi Modern Poets in Focus 5* (London: Corgi, 1973), p. 60.

36. *London Magazine*, Dec. 1961, p. 7.

37. Letter to Ross, dated Oct. 29, 1962, from Vienna (HRC).

38. To Ross, May 5, 1963, from Vienna (HRC).

39. These and following descriptions by Spencer of life in Vienna are taken from private correspondence dated October and November 1962 (AH).

40. G. S. Fraser, 'For Bernard Spencer,' *TLS*, Sept. 27, 1963, p. 746.

41. George Seferis, 'The Greek Poems of Lawrence Durrell,' trans. Anthony Tyrrell, *Labrys*, July 1979, p. 91.

42. In a letter to the editor, dated Sept. 25, 1978.

43. Obituary, *The Times*, Sept. 13, 1963, p. 14.

44. Robin Fedden, 'In Memoriam Bernard Spencer,' *Poetry Book Society Bulletin*, December 1963.

45. *The Poet Speaks*, pp. 236–37.

46. 'Bernard Spencer Writes,' *Poetry Book Society Bulletin*, June 1963.

47. G. S., 'Mathaios Pascalis His Ideas About Poems,' *Personal Landscape*, vol. 2, pt. 3 (1944), p. 2.

48. *The Poet Speaks*, p. 237.

AEGEAN ISLANDS
AND OTHER POEMS

Allotments: April

Cobbled with rough stone which rings my tread
The path twists through the squared allotments.
Blinking to glimpse the lark in the warming sun,
In what sense am I joining in
Such a hallooing, rousing April day,
Now that the hedges are so gracious and
Stick out at me moist buds, small hands, their opening scrolls and
    fans?

Lost to some of us the festival joy
At the bursting of the tomb, the seasonal mystery,
God walking again who lay all winter
As if in those long barrows built in the fields
To keep the root-crops warm. On squires' lawns
The booted dancers twirl. But what I hear
A spade slice in pebbled earth, swinging the nigger-coloured loam.

And the love-songs, the mediæval grace,
The fluting lyrics, 'The only pretty ring-time,'
These have stopped singing. For love detonates like sap
Up into the limbs of men and bears all the seasons
And the starving and the cutting and hunts terribly through lives
To find its peace. But April comes as
Beast-smell flung from the fields, the hammers, the loud-speaking
    weir.

The rough voices of boys playing by the hedge
As manly as possible, their laughter, the big veins
Sprawled over the beet-leaf, light-red fires
Of flower pots heaped by the huts; they make a pause in
The wireless voice repeating pacts, persecutions,

1

And imprisonments and deaths and heaped violent deaths,
Impersonal now as figures in the city news.

Behind me, the town curves. Its parapeted edge,
With its burnt look, guards towards the river.
The worry about money, the eyeless work
Of those who do not believe, real poverty,
The sour doorways of the poor; April which
Delights the trees and fills the roads to the South,
Does not deny or conceal. Rather it adds

What more I am; excites the deep glands
And warms my animal bones as I go walking
Past the allotments and the singing water-meadows
Where hooves of cattle have plodded and cratered, and
Watch today go up like a single breath
Holding in its applause at masts of height
Two elms and their balanced attitude like dancers, their arms like
    dancers.

A Hand

The human hand lying on my hand
(The wrist had a gilt bangle on)
Wore its print of personal lines
Took breath as lungs and leaves and
Tasted in the skin our sun.

The living palm and the near-to-bone:
Fine animal hairs where the light shone.

The handed mole to its earth, the stoat to the dark
And this flesh to its nature nervously planned;
To dig love's heart till everything is shown,
To hunt, to hold its mark
– This loved hand.

Plains as Large as Europe

Plains as large as Europe is
Where each of us walks and is alone
In my giving a cigarette to a passer
As anyone might have done
Were clearly known and shown.

But there was real and final friending
Going beyond the mere gentleness
Of little need and little favour.
For us who would soon part
In the sea-wind whirled street

For me who had come three hundred miles;
A certainty of vaster love, and a hunger
Burlier to bind us simply as men
Than any home river
Or the grass of graves there.

There was no Instruction Given

There was no instruction given
But closed faces of elders seen at school
Were voices blabbing out some clue:
We were children and learned amo,
But the years passed and the bells stopped;
In the morning, 'What do you mean to do
Now all things are crumbling new?'

Another age hammers out amo
With love and the very hills breaking and new:
And it's, Learn – if you can – upon the quick
How the stubborn break inside like bones.
How once the wheel swung true
And there were our hearts, there were Reigate and London:
Now ghosts; or all trampled new.

Houses are Uniformed

Houses are uniformed in black
Here wage-work lies heavier;
I think their colour, and I walk
Asking my way to the memory
Of your flesh and loved behaviour.

In a room after dinner
Manoeuvering Italy or France
And the bookie-governments backing a winner,
Voices rise. Near-despair
Grits on tired nonchalance.

I imagine your voice, but I hear
Voices at some different time;
'I work, I take pay, but there
Is no more good in the work. Our life
Has moved, has another name.'

Lives flat, neither sweet nor sour
Ascetic faces in the street.
A nervous haunting left from the war
Confessed at midnight over drinks;
It is our passion these hit.

If we could leave the brain
Or some deputy in place
To bear the voices, measure the stain
– But the same scene is love's scene
Its Alexandria or Greece.

A contrast passing the spoken
Gives thought of you
A journey visa-ed and broken,
Not quick as a telephone
Or the hand that stings the bone through.

Touch of skin, touch of hair
What domes wheel above and grate?
Into what marsh air
Spring love's smoothed-underground
Flowers, its unthumbed shape?

Evasions

How many times have you smiled a reckoning smile
Either when there was some question of money
Or to humour one of the dead who live around?
– Oh, but that's been going on since the world began.

How many times face to face with your lover
Have you housed apart contracted with fear and cunning
Hidden from the body and that violent weather?
– Oh but that's been going on since the fall of man.

How many times smelling the smell of poverty
Have you tired and turned for good to your cornfield and garden
(And cornfield and garden grew foul pods and rotted)?
– Oh but that's been going on since the world began.

Portrait of a Woman and Others

Let me out of my life
Said the line skewing
From eye up brow, renewing
Always, but most in sleep.
How long must I keep
Hard skull and knees,
She said, and serve these
Like a loathing wife?
Free me from my body's sloughing
With its tireless tide-measure,
From the rest and the whip of pleasure.
Let me out of my life.

She never breathed this out.

I wonder, now it is Spring,
Throwing like beams each thing
The tiger and the daffodil
And hunting on that hill;
Though rock holds its great head
Opposed, you would think, and dead true
Does all nerve and all grace
Turn also back its face?

It can be we are not alone,
Contradicted by the X-ray bone.
It can be that each thing keeps
As we do, deep among deeps
A will not for winter and such sleeps
But for what really reaps.

A Cold Night

Thick wool is muslin tonight, and the wire
Wind scorches stone-cold colder. Boys
Tremble at counters of shops. The world
Gets lopped at the radius of my fire.

Only for a moment I think of those
Whom the weather leans on under the sky;
Newsmen with placards by the river's skirt,
Stamping, or with their crouching pose,

The whores; the soldiery who lie
Round wounded Madrid; those of less hurt
Who cross that bridge I crossed today
Where the waves snap white as broken plates

And the criss-cross girders hammer a grill
Through which, instead of flames, wind hates.

I turn back to my fire. Which I must.
I am not God or a crazed woman.
And one needs time too to sit in peace
Opposite one's girl, with food, fire, light,

And do the work one's own blood heats,
Or talk, and forget about the winter
– This season, this century – and not be always
Opening one's doors on the pitiful streets

Of Europe, not always think of winter, winter, like a
        hammering rhyme
For then everything is drowned by the rising wind,
        everything is done against Time.

Part of Plenty

When she carries food to the table and stoops down
– Doing this out of love – and lays soup with its good
Tickling smell, or fry winking from the fire
And I look up, perhaps from a book I am reading
Or other work: there is an importance of beauty
Which can't be accounted for by there and then,
And attacks me, but not separately from the welcome
Of the food, or the grace of her arms.

When she puts a sheaf of tulips in a jug
And pours in water and presses to one side
The upright stems and leaves that you hear creak,
Or loosens them, or holds them up to show me,
So that I see the tangle of their necks and cups
With the curls of her hair, and the body they are held
Against, and the stalk of the small waist rising
And flowering in the shape of breasts;

Whether in the bringing of the flowers or the food
She offers plenty, and is part of plenty,
And whether I see her stooping, or leaning with the flowers,
What she does is ages old, and she is not simply,
No, but lovely in that way.

Cage

That canary measures out its prison.
To perch as quick as camera-shutter, perch
Is left for the little hoop where it can swing.
The next thing is the wiry wall, and cling
With tail and twiggy feet. Then back to perch.
Then it fluffs out its throat and sings, content,
As I can judge, born barred.
There follows its tour of the globe, watch till you tire;
Perch, hoop, and wire,
Perch, wire and hoop.
A minute shows its life, but I watch hard,
Fascinated, who have to write
An account of myself in five hundred words
For a sociological group.
Neat fists of wire clench around caged birds;
Human cages narrow or retreat.
The dead laws of a stiffening State
Shoot up forests of oppressive iron;
The shouting of each military saviour
Bolts bars of iron;
Money, houses, shudder into iron.
Within that fence I am whatever I am.
And I carry my inherited wish to be free,
And my inherited wish to be tied for ever,
As natural to me as my body.
Unlike the bird in the cage, feather to wire,
I lean out some hours,
I lunge to left, I lunge out to right
And hit no bars that way, only mist's pretence;
I cannot estimate my powers.
But, measuring man and bird,
In this respect the likeness stays:
Much of my life will go to exploring my fence.

Ill

Expectant at the country gate the lantern. On the night
Its silks of light strained. Lighted upper window.
'Is it you who sent for me?' The two go in
To where the woman lies ill, upstairs, out of sight.

I hear sky softly smother to earth in rain,
As I sit by the controls and the car's burning dials.
And always the main-road traffic searching, searching the horizons.
Then those sounds knifed by the woman's Ah! of pain.

Who dreamed this; the dark folding murderer's hands round the lamps?
The rain blowing growth to rot? Lives passed beneath a ritual
That tears men's ghosts and bodies; the few healers
With their weak charms, moving here and there among the lamps?

A *Thousand Killed*

I read of a thousand killed.
And am glad because the scrounging imperial paw
Was there so bitten:
As a man at elections is thrilled
When the results pour in, and the North goes with him
And the West breaks in the thaw.

(That fighting was a long way off.)

Forgetting therefore an election
Being fought with votes and lies and catch-cries
And orator's frowns and flowers and posters' noise,
Is paid for with cheques and toys:
Wars the most glorious
Victory-winged and steeple-uproarious
. . . With the lives, burned-off,
Of young men and boys.

Suburb Factories

White as a drawing on white paper
The architect built the tall
Suburb factories,
Compact as a liner admired from the littered beach
Gaunt like the ward of a hospital.

And when he sunk their roots among
The places of spare trees
The huts and the wastes,
To stare down the polished arterial road,
And to peer across the chimneys,

Made the big concrete mushrooms grow,
Towers with gland-heads;
He edged to the cliff
The doomed life of the villas; fastidious streets,
Men signed with their fathers' manual trades,

Their faces curiously primmed and clenched
If perhaps they can leap above the memory
Of those scorned trades.
Stamping, the concrete brushes down their fences,
It brings drilled crowds, small property.

Changes though; change is the air; roofscape
Touches some nerve, and the lost
Sinking scream
Of electric trains touches it, and white masonry
Springs up like a fire, but strikes like frost.

Waiting

To sit in the heavily curtained, old ladyish, waiting-room
While upstairs the gloved surgeon operates on a loved one,
Imagined as candle-still and unlike life, in the brilliant
Gas-sweet theatre. To listen to the clock's 'Doubt, doubt,' and to hear
The metal of the knives made ready; and not to know any news;
       That helpless fear.

Is it like that bad dream of knives, our counting the years
Our listening to rumours until the guns begin and our volted
Delight in creating, our love, our famous words, and the personal
Order of our lives is devoured when our streets become a furnace?
I think so in times of despair, and the good in our random culture
       Woundable as a man is.

Yet know that from our crisis leads no white stair to a shut
Door and the deftness of another's hands. What sickness threatens
Our freedom to lounge in the green world, to be happy beneath the
Clocks of its cities we largely know. If we live we have the pride
To be capable of action, to speak out plainly. The wise and passionate
       Are on our side.

How Must we Live?

'How must we live?' From the caress, the shadow
Of that mother-Peace giver of our tongues, our eyes,
We advance, the sowers of cities. Back there
      We see rise

Her image, the firm-footed, as men have used
Over harbours, seen the first and last. Now
Built up the sky by the old philosophy
      The stone breasts, stone brow.

Blood in unquiet; 'From that nature we were born.'
When we look forward, knowledge will not serve;
The immense only is seen, as who from a height
      Views the globe's curve.

Faces arrest us and the particular pity;
Wings, water, move us. But a deeper way
'What have we to live by?' beats back into brain
      And cannot be frowned away.

My Sister

The old man bearded with illness weakens upstairs.
My sister who is great with child
Speaks of our early long days
In the house with the fig-tree in the garden;
We speak of what the nurses taught
And the schools that teach our class,
Of what friends we had,
Of theatres, difference that money made.
My sister great with child, and the old man dying upstairs.

Across our stroke-by-stroke built-up picture
And, since, our eating with new friends
And turning upon new living-ways
As if exploring a turning stream,
Our laughing, travelling at different times;
Memory of gross South and North,
Making big slash and score
With asleep, hurting, and death and birth
Scrawls in comment which way the master-winds wear.

Aegean Islands 1940–41

Where white stares, smokes or breaks,
Thread white, white of plaster and of foam,
Where sea like a wall falls;
Ribbed, lionish coast,
The stony islands which blow into my mind
More often than I imagine my grassy home;

To sun one's bones beside the
Explosive, crushed-blue, nostril-opening sea
(The weaving sea, splintered with sails and foam,
Familiar of famous and deserted harbours,
Of coins with dolphins on and fallen pillars.)

To know the gear and skill of sailing,
The drenching race for home and the sail-white houses,
Stories of Turks and smoky ikons,
Cry of the bagpipe, treading
Of the peasant dancers;

The dark bread
The island wine and the sweet dishes;
All these were elements in a happiness
More distant now than any date like '40,
A. D. or B.C., ever can express.

Greek Excavations

Over the long-shut house
Which earth, not keys kept under watch,
I prod with a stick and down comes rattling soil
Into the dug out room;
And pottery comes down,
Hard edges of drinking vessels, jars for oil,
Mere kitchen stuff, rubbish of red or brown,
Stubble of conquests

– And I suddenly discover this discovered town.
The wish of the many, their abused trust,
Blows down here in a little dust,
So much unpainted clay;
The minimum wish
For the permanence of the basic things of a life,
For children and friends and having enough to eat
And the great key of a skill;
The life the generals and the bankers cheat.

Peering for coin or confident bust
Or vase in bloom with the swiftness of horses,
My mind was never turned the way
Of the classic of the just and the unjust.
I was looking for things which have a date,
And less of the earth's weight,
When I broke this crust.

Salonika June 1940

My end of Europe is at war. For this
My lamp-launched giant shadow seems to fall
Like a bad thought upon this ground at peace,
Being the shadow of the shadow of a war.
What difference if I wish good luck to these foreigners, my hosts?
Talking with my friends stand ghosts.

Specially the lives that here in the crook of this bay
At the paws of its lionish hills are lived as I know;
The dancing, the bathing, the order of the market, and as day
Cools into night, boys playing in the square;
Island boats and lemon-peel tang and the timeless café crowd,
And the outcry of dice on wood:

I would shut the whole if I could out of harm's way
As one shuts a holiday photo away in a desk,
Or shuts one's eyes. But not by this brilliant bay,
Nor in Hampstead now where leaves are green,
Any more exists a word or a lock which gunfire may not break,
Or a love whose range it may not take.

Delos

Wealth came by water to this farmless island;
Dolphins with backs like bows swim in mosaic
Floors where the Greek sea-captains piled up money;
And the jagged circular patterns spin with the rush of
The impetus and fling of waves.

Steps go down to the port. And in this area
You could buy corn and oil or men and women.
Above on the windy hill Leto the human
Bore her birth pains, gave two gods to a legend
Glittering and loveless like the sea.

Slavery, we know, was not of the market only.
Here specially were rich and poor, priests and their pennies.
Imperial slavery we know. But the salt Aegean
Rolled waves of flame and killing, quarrels of aliens,
Till life here burst and was quiet.

In the boulevards of these dead you will think of violence,
Holiness and violence, violence of sea that is bluer
Than blue eyes are; violence of sun and its worship;
Of money and its worship. And it was here by the breakers
That strangers asked for the truth.

Base Town

Winter's white guard continual on the hills;
The wind savaging from the stony valleys
And the unseen front. And always the soldiers going,
Soldiers and lorries beating the streets of cobble,
Like blood to where a wound is flowing.

War took friends, lights and names away. Clapped down
Shutters on windows' welcome. Brought those letters
Which wished to say so much they dared not say.
The proud and feminine ships in the harbour roads
Turned to a North-East grey.

Curious the intimacy we felt with Them;
We moved our meals to fit Their raids; we read
Their very hand across each bomb-slashed wall.
Their charred plane fallen in the cratered square
Held twisted in it all

Their work, Their hate, Their failure. Prisoners
Bearded and filthy, had bones, eyes and hair
Like other men in need. But dead like snow,
Cold like those racing winds or sirens' grief,
Was the hate which struck no blow:

The fear of speaking was a kind of tic
Pulling at the eyes. If stranger drank with stranger
It seemed thief drank with thief. Was it only every
Night, the fall of the early and lampless dark?
I remember it so often. And the lie,
The twist of reason,
The clever rumour planted in the nerves,
The dossier infecting like a coccus;
All these became for us the town, the season.

These, and the knowledge that to die,
Some stony miles north of our wintering
Was a more ordinary thing.

Death of an Airman

Dancer's naked foot so earthly planted
Limbs tall and turned to music of drums; all growth,
Grass, fountaining palm exulting and vertical,
      Dance his fair hair, his youth.

For when you tread delight as if a wire
And when your roots in the dark finger earth's springs
Your strength has an understanding that includes
Those shot-down wings.

Letters

Letters, like blood along a weakening body
move fainter round our map. On dangerous wings,
on darkness-loving keels they go, so longed for;
but say no memorable things.

The 'dear' and 'darling' and the 'yours for ever'
are relics of a style. But most appears
mere rambling notes; passion and tenderness
fall like a blot or a burst of tears.

Now public truths are scarcer currency,
what measure for the personal truth? how can
this ink and paper coursing continents
utter the clothed or the naked man?

Libyan Front

Cratered the land, unploughed, unsown, unfamiliar as a star
       Libyan front
Routine and dirt and story telling are triggered to something far
Night is Death's day when he sees best and when his appointments are
       Libyan front
Sand, our metaphor for time and waste, is all the world and its springs
       Libyan front
Very distant the feet that dance, the lifted silver and the strings
Poets and lovers and men of power are troops and no such things
       Libyan front.

Egyptian Delta

Rhyme for the runnels feeling among the crops
like fingers stroked through hair:
rhyme for the floating bare-foot walkers at evening,
the upright women with burdened heads who wear
five thousand years like a dress:
water wheel, rope and harness, where
the powerful ox with dancer's step goes round,
and his lifted eyes bound.

Be glad for taps and nozzles and water flowering,
the sozzling gardens drunk:
blossoms catching fire like a match's flaring,
semaphore of madman flags from bough and trunk:
eyes from the mud, and laughing,
filth and hunger steady as the sun. And sunk
somewhere in all a patience of this ground,
like the blind ox's round.

Pulling through nations, fountained further than thought,
the river with a breeze on its back
suddenly lifts your hair with coolness. Be
measureless because of water. Move through lack,
through sands, prodigious harvest.
There is an excellence of losing track,
of being no longer a person or sad. Being drowned,
being water, hooves, and their round.

Acre

In Acre it wasn't simply the peeping alleys,
the cobbles and the grave and Frankish gate:
towers stone by stone surrendering
all their Crusading darkness up to the sun;
though these could touch or fascinate:
not squares chattering with colours,
the long and leaping boats heeled on their sides;
melons and nets, and under arches the Eastern
sea gay as a scarf:
then the Turkish mosque fountaining delicate
columns like sheltered thoughts.
                                    But not these nor
the useful whitened petrol tins
tracing the metalled high-road, nor the Arab
cemetery grieving for a few decades
where the town flung its rubbish.
                                    Any such symbols,
or the whole jangled argument of eras
and lusts and cries for justice, might set fire to
the poet's immoderate, promiscuous love.

Frontier

A turn in the road. The bare and echoing shed.
A few men armed. Long tables for the Customs.
And there in the country grass some chickens fed,
and children were making a private world with their calling
where there were trees and a house. A clerk
with reddened eyes,
slowly turned marriage, travel and birth to paper,
like indexing the dead:
released one waiting figure towards the bed
of a lover, so long starved for, morning and night;
others a hundred miles to an epidemic,
to power, to a famine, to be quite alone:

gravely would write, though some slipped by like spies
with wild thoughts in their head,
in columns for them; in columns too for those
who saw in absolute file, in moody gun,
a permanence, a being somehow right,
like rocks, like turns in the road, like children's cries.

Cairo Restaurant

Light thrown
such as to trace the bone:
the few electric lamps in the little room
examining the heartless things of a face,
brow or measurable fall of cheek bone;
digging a cave to lair the desperate lies
or urgent witness of the eyes:
falling elsewhere on objects with no grace,
the narrow restaurant, its glass and wood,
rough service and rough food:
the welcome that a little money buys
out of the hungry East.

Lights burning. Expectation of news. A thought
of a stable, of an inn,
an upper room.

Again in the Eastern province of an iron empire,
being is dirtied by a banker's thumb,
bread is once more the bread we merely use:
eye and instinct cannot choose;
we are also born for a message to begin,
a narrow room, a tomb,
a portent and a danger that may give
a grace and a meaning; our bread too must live.

The Ship

The simple beach and the sea. And separate things
lie on this openness as on a hand;
sea-coloured tents, a boat upon its side,
Scarlet of flags, a children's see-saw, swings,
like elementary shapes a child has drawn;
and the mind grasps them in a stride.

Very deliberate, like a mannequin,
a full-rigged ship goes South,
and lets you tell for half an hour or more
how hollowed sails and keen unhurried bows
can be so lucid and so brave,
poet nor painter find one jot to add,
not the hairbreadth of a line,
wing or turning wave.

No wonder mind should find this scenery bland
as lotions are to eyes;
our loves being mostly natives of a land
mountainous, hung with forests, loud with storms:
and our thoughts climb
to light like things the digger's spade has struck,
a broken dish, a ring,
confused with dark and roots and time.

Behaviour of Money

Money was once well known, like a townhall or the sky
or a river East and West, and you lived one side or the other;
Love and Death dealt shocks,
but for all the money that passed, the wise man knew his brother.

But money changed. Money came jerking roughly alive;
went battering round the town with a boozy, zigzag tread.
A clear case for arrest;
and the crowds milled and killed for the pound notes that he shed.

And the town changed, and the mean and the little lovers of gain
inflated like a dropsy, and gone were the courtesies
that eased the market day;
saying, 'buyer' and 'seller' was saying, 'enemies.'

The poor were shunted nearer to beasts. The cops recruited.
The rich became a foreign community. Up there leaped
quiet folk gone nasty,
quite strangely distorted, like a photograph that has slipped.

Hearing the drunken roars of Money from down the street,
'What's to become of us?' the people in bed would cry:
'And oh, the thought strikes chill;
what's to become of the world if Money should suddenly die?

Should suddenly take a toss and go down crack on his head?
If the dance suddenly finished, if they stopped the runaway bus,
if the trees stopped racing away?
If our hopes come true and he dies, what's to become of us?

Shall we recognise each other, crowding around the body?
And as we go stealing off in search of the town we have known
– what a job for the Sanitary Officials;
the sprawled body of Money, dead, stinking, alone!'

Will X contrive to lose the weasel look in his eyes?
Will the metal go out of the voice of Y? Shall we all turn back
to men, like Circe's beasts?
Or die? Or dance in the street the day that the world goes crack?

Yachts on the Nile

Like air on skin, coolness of yachts at mooring,
a white, flung handful;
fresh as a girl at her rendezvous, and wearing
frou-frou names, Suzy, Yvette or Gaby,
lipped by the current, uttering
the gay conversation of their keels.

Lovely will be their hesitant leaving of
the shore for the full stream,
fingering the breeze down out of the sky; then leaning
as a player leans his cheek to the violin
— that strange repose of power —
and the race will hold them like a legend.

Terrible their perfection: and theirs I saw
like clouds covering the Solent
when I was a boy: and all those sails that dip
ages back in the hardly waking mind;
white visitors of islands,
runners on the turf of rivers.

What these ask with their conquering look and speed
written in their bodies like birds,
is our ecstasy, our tasting as if a dish,
magnificence of hazard, cunning of the tiller-hand,
a freedom: and it is by something
contrary in being human

That I look for a distant river, a distant woman,
and how she carried her head:
the great release of the race interns me here . . .
and it may be, too, we are born with some nostalgia
to make the migration of sails
and wings a crying matter.

Olive Trees

The dour thing in olive trees
is that their trunks are stooped like never dying crones,
and they camp where roads climb, and drink with dust and stones.

The pleasant thing is how in the heat
their plumage brushes the sight with a bird's-wing feeling:
and perhaps the gold of their oil is mild with dreams of healing.

The cold thing is how they were
there at the start of us; and one grey look surveyed
the builder imagining the city, the historian with his spade.

The warm thing is that they are
first promise of the South to waking travellers:
of the peacock sea, and the islands and their boulder-lumbered spurs.

The Building of the House

The building of the house became a part
of all our lives; how old it looked at first,
like an anatomy dissected:
how some inverted surgery fleshed it, nursed
features from out of clay and eyes to see;
and how the builders worked and all their gear,
the bucket, brick and rubble and the art
of ladder, hod or rope,
were the remoter touches, cool in feeling,
against whose background what was memorable
showed sad or smiling.

Then startlingly the house was finished, and stood
more weather-worthy than our bodies could:
and for two lifetimes' interval
no one would see exactly what we had seen,
towards the bridge and the wood.

Why was this something we had not foreseen?
By what sharp argument of brick or stone
had we now first to love even those hours
– and maybe find them worst to lose –
which, passing, never touched us to the bone?

Peasant Festival

All day they had worshipped at the Virgin's picture
and now they camped, their families and their beasts,
with harness and piled fruit and mothers suckling
around the little mountain church, or moved
among the stalls, where tradesmen cried.
The petrol flares lit light and dark; and starlight
and the blind peaks and resin bleeding forests
cupped them above the plain.

What brought them riding here were not our customs,
and yet it was good to share their food with them
– wine from the village and white cheese – and know them
across some hundred years with their high boots
and great moustaches. And their songs,
love songs and bawdy songs at fall of night,
said after-things which rang like that cold air
as, one voice sang
under the dark of the trees; 'If I entered Heaven
and did not find you there and your little breasts
I should understand nothing.'

Egyptian Dancer at Shubra

At first we heard the jingling of her ornaments
as she delayed beyond the trap of light,
and glimpsed her lingering pretence
her bare feet and the music were at difference:
and then the strings grew wild and drew her in.

And she came soft as paws and danced desire at play
or triumphing desire, and locked her hands
stretched high, and in the dance's sway
hung like a body to be flogged; then wrenched away,
or was a wave from breasts down to the knees.

And as the music built to climax and she leaned
naked in her dancing skirt, and was supreme,
her dance's stormy argument
had timid workday things for all environment;
men's awkward clothes and chairs her skin exclaimed against.

Passed On

Some of his messages were personal
almost as his lost face; they showed he knew
about their pets, the life that went on beating
in desks and scrapbooks, and each particle

of the family language: the young engineer,
who had put khaki on and died in the mud,
at times would almost touch them.
                                        Yet he was
(But how?) the sing-song spirit-gospeller;

the irrelevance, the baby-talk and spout
of 'Vera,' the Control; and stagey things,
a bell, a violin, an Indian chief;
even what crashed the furniture about.

But then he was their son. That love, that birth
made the old couple blind enough to bear
the medium's welcome, taking no offence,
and haunt his room that opened clean off earth.

In an Auction Room

How many deaths and partings spilled
this jumble in an upper room;
and every chair or mirror filled
with elbowing and smell of lives:
the gloom
of this tall wardrobe stopped the sun
entering a home; the great brass bed
stood in its throne-room, and its springs
and shining arms are crammed like mines
with regal illness and with love:
the terrible settee
with worn red flowers, the table de nuit,
the picture with the little man
walking the infinite road
to a West of gold;
these have all been (and are to be)
loves truer than our human mould,
or desperate walls
flung up against the shock of things,
what has no name; or growing old.

Sarcophagi

Excellent ritual of oils, of anointing,
office of priests;
everything was paid before these dead put on
the armless dress of their sarcophagi,
lying down in Phoenicia,

pillowing their heavy sculptured heads, their broad
foreheads like rides of sand, the rock of the chin,
the mouth, the simple map of the face, the carved
hair in full sail.

Surrender of sunlight and market and the white
loops of the coast,
was simply a journey, a bargain rigid as stone:
though youth took passage.

Stretched by the salt and echoing roads to the West
twenty-six bargain-makers of Phoenicia;
twenty-six dead with wide eyes,
confident of harbour.

WITH LUCK LASTING

The Beginning

Its pale walls partly clambered on by creeper,
it slowly disentangles to the sight
out of the hill as you drive past the Bosphorus;
the castle, where the straits veer narrowest.

That acre of turret and bow-slit was enough
to start a war with. When it once was built
Mehmet and Asia marched out to the conquest
of Constaninople, while the Christian West
dallied, debated, lost their cause.

It was the beginning. It sealed the narrows off.
But in the end the castle grew tremendous;
changed maps, slew thousands, put out like an eye
world-renowned mural work of crowns and thrones and wings,
realized an age-old nightmare,
and ranged along the City's dusty sky-line
the muezzins' pointed towers like lances lifted.

Delicate Grasses

Delicate grasses blowing in the wind,
grass out of cracks among tiered seats of stone
where a Greek theatre swarmed with audience,
till Time's door shut upon
the stir, the eloquence.

A hawk waiting above the enormous plain,
lying upon the nothing of the air,
a hawk who turns at some sky-wave or lull
this way, and after there
as dial needles prowl.

Cool water jetting from a drinking fountain
in crag-lands, miles from any peopled spot,
year upon year with its indifferent flow;
sound that is and is not;
the wet stone trodden low.

There is no name for such strong liberation;
I drift their way; I need what their world lends;
then, chilled by one thought further still than those,
I swerve towards life and friends
before the trap-fangs close.

Notes by a Foreigner

Their opaque, restless eyes,
the last place you will find a clue to this town;
eyes that face yours or hunger past you,
darknesses cut from a woman's evening gown.

Encounters with frequent phantoms,
women whose beauty lays a hand on your gut:
the sound of the impetuous language,
blurred as if the tongue still savoured fruit.

Your wish to build them all
into one vision, with traffic bells, the fine
knives of the whistles, and the blind,
tapping to the world like caught souls down a mine.

The shuffle of evening crowds
past cinema lights; each sixteenth-century square
where the bronze kings and heroes rein
their grave war-stallions back: and everywhere

Blocks without hope going up,
windowless brick down two gaunt sides, that back
on wastes of sand and dazing lion-light
through which walk women in their mourning black.

Illusion, your old failure
to see except as a foreigner. There is just
a sense in which your town never
was true, for all its trams and banks and dust

-doomed sunsets like the hell
over a town bombarded, and for all
that light that stays a half hour more
as though mad cocks had given the dawn a call,

The echo-light no town
(of this at least you are sure), can parallel;
when things mean more yet fade, like places
you half remember, a now-not-beating bell.

43

From my Window

Now when the University students have abandoned
their game of bowls in the garden, with their cries of 'Two' or 'Six'
and the evening sky goes soured milk,

There are left the brightening windows of the rich owners of flats;
their meaningless finny gestures, dumb departures and entries;
a deaf man's theatre twenty times.

And quite indifferent towards the students or the rich
there are left the children of the poor, playing tag on a sandy waste,
and miles off southward ring the trams.

Alone on a building site a watchdog stalks by the fire,
wooed and repulsed by the jump-away flames, or raises its head
at a barking that chips a hole in distance.

Mediterranean Suburbs

Sunset; the streets of flats, new and forbidding;
on the left in the vacant site a block is rising,
ground plan and girders like a giant doodle;
opposite, waiting for its history,
forty blank eyes, another stares, unfinished.

Here in their heavy homes there live the solid
such as those passing now, the Father strutting
with legs apart, Mama in her striped furs,
two woollied stubborn children dragging after.

Reject of neighbouring streets, then questioning ours,
the sad and stammering music of a pipe;
and now its tall and scarecrow player turns
the corner like the grotesque of some need
we had forgotten that we were starving from,
or promise we have broken. Empty houses,
houses for next year, evening, restless houses.
Dressed in a city's shabbiness he walks
under the wild guess of that new-starred sky.

Fluted Armour

Bored and humbled by every disintegrating day,
because, meaningless, the wine-glass and the storm-cloud stayed
particular things:
having, as everyone must, lost my way;
I went to the National Gallery to trade
a confusion of particulars
for what you might call a philosophy, for
the world-gaze of the great Italians and was not
disappointed returning by Charing Cross Road, dazed
by particular things:
the narrowed eyes and caught breath of the archers in
    Pollaiuolo's 'San Sebastian',
the smiling lips of Bronzino's 'Venus',
and in Piero di Cosimo's 'Florentine General'
the cold smite of the fluted armour my finger-tips had grazed.

Out of Sleep

Surfacing out of sleep she feared
voices in the sky talking
with thick tongues. Night flashed
brightening her eyelids. Yet as panic cleared
she knew those voices never spoke the harsh
brogue of the guns. And then the rain
sighed in the leaves; it was thunder.
The rain said, hush.

It has been peace in our world a year:
what worse-than-memories seep
to infect our nights with fear
up from the angers of that other war,
ours copy here?
What towns burn on what darker coast of sleep,
how many histories deep?

A *Spring Wind*

Spring shakes the windows; doors whang to,
the sky moves half in dark and half
shining like knives: upon this table
Elytis' poems lie
uttering the tangle of sea, the 'breathing caves'
and the fling of Aegean waves.

I am caught here in this scattering, vagrant season
where telephones ring;
and all Greece goes through me
as the wind goes searching through the city streets.
Greece, I have so much loved you
out of all reason;
that this unquiet time
its budding and its pride
the news and the nostalgia of Spring
swing towards you their tide:

Towards the windmills on the islands;
Alefkandra loved by winds,
luminous with foam and morning, Athens,
her blinded marble heads,
her pepper-trees, the bare heels of her girls,
old songs that bubble up from where thought starts,
Greek music treading like the beat of hearts;
haunted Seferis, smiling, playing with beads.

And since especially at this time
statues and blossoms, birth and death require
we give account of manhood and of youth,
the wind that whirls through London also rings
with the bang and echo of the Easter gun,
as in days gone,
from where the pilgrims' torches climb
over a darkening town
to set that bony peak Lykahvetoss,
Athens, and all the opening year on fire.

On a Carved Axle-Piece from a Sicilian Cart

The village craftsman stirred his bravest yellow
and (all the carpentry and carving done)
put the last touches to his newest cart,
until no playing-card had brighter panels;
with crested knights in armour, king and crown,
Crusaders slaughtering infidels, and crimson
where the blood laves:
and took his paintpot to that part
around the axle where a Southern memory
harking back out of Christendom, imagined
a chariot of glory
and Aphrodite riding wooden waves.

So some tanned peasant paid his money down
and till the years
put a full-stop to him or his purchase, jaunted
half around Sicily with wood for the fire,
long muscat grapes
or tangerines for the market in the town.
Thus answering, as his fathers' fathers had,
those metaphysical gaps and fears
which drain the blood of the age or drive it mad;
the 'why are we guilty?' and the 'who must punish?'

– With a salty way of speech; with tasselled harness
with a cart to match the sea and all the flowers;
with Roger the Christian and Palermo towers;
and in between the dusty wheels
the Queen of Love in a yellow gown,
featured like a peasant child,
her three red horses rearing from the foam
and their carved manes blown wild.

The Boats

Five boats beside the lake,
pulled bows first up the shore; how hard it is
to draw them, from each angle changing, elegant:
their feminine poise, the 'just so' lifting sweep
of the light timbers round the flanks sucked thin
into the thirsty bows;
                            the same or nearly
as makes no difference, since men settled first
near these magnolias, lived the different life
that is always the same; fished, traded, hammered, gossiped
wanted their food and wine, appeased the Powers,
meditated journeys
or turned and turned in their minds some woman's image,
lost or distant.
                            Near this bench and the keels
someone has scratched in the dust the name ELSA.

At *Courmayeur*

This climbers' valley with its wayside shrines
(the young crowned Mother and her dying flowers)
became our theme for weeks. Do you remember
the letters that we wrote and how we planned
the journey there and chose our hotel; ours
was to be one 'among the pines'?

Guesses went wide; but zigzag past that ridge
the road climbs from the Roman town; there stand
the glittering peaks, and one, the God, immensely
tossing the clouds around his shoulders; here
are what you asked for, summer pastures and
an air with glaciers in its edge.

Under all sounds is mountain water falling;
at night, the river seems to draw much closer;
darling, how did you think I could forget you,
you who for ever stayed behind? Your absence
comes back as hard as rocks. Just now it was
those hangdown flowers that meant recalling.

In a Foreign Hospital

Valleys away in the August dark the thunder
roots and tramples: lightning sharply prints
for an instant trees, hills, chimneys on the night.
We lie here in our similar rooms with the white
furniture, with our bit of Death inside us
(nearer than that Death our whole life lies under);
the man in the next room with the low voice,
the brown-skinned boy, the child among its toys
and I and others. Against my bedside light
a small green insect flings itself with a noise
tiny and regular, a 'tink; tink, tink'.

A Nun stands rustling by, saying good night,
hooded and starched and smiling with her kind
lifeless, religious eyes. 'Is there anything
you want?' – 'Sister, why yes, so many things:'
England is somewhere far away to my right
and all Your letter promised; days behind
my left hand or my head (or a whole age)
are dearer names and easier beds than here.
But since tonight must lack for all of these
I am free to keep my watch with images,
a bare white room, the World, an insect's rage,
and if I am lucky, find some link, some link.

Regent's Park Terrace

The noises round my house. On cobbles bounding
Victorian-fashioned drays laden with railway goods;
their hollow sound like stones in rolling barrels:
the stony hoofing of dray horses.

Further, the trains themselves; among them the violent,
screaming like frightened animals, clashing metal;
different the pompous, the heavy breathers, the aldermen,
of those again which speed with the declining
sadness of crying along the distant routes
knitting together weathers and dialects.

Between these noises the little teeth
of a London silence.

Finally the lions grumbling over the park,
angry in the night hours,
cavernous as though their throats were openings up from the earth:
hooves, luggage, engines, tumbrils, lions,
hollow noises, noises of travel, hourly these unpick
the bricks of a London terrace, make the ear
their road, and have their audience in whatever
hearing the heart or the deep of the belly owns.

Letter Home

Walk on a fallen sky;
tread softer on a blue paste of dropped jacaranda petals:
that sentry's face and hands
are carpentered from the same dark wood as his rifle butt:
past gardens and armed men
is a street number to find, 58, 57, 56:
the heat follows me around
like an overcoat in a dream; a ship's siren from the river
trembles the air with sorrows and names of iron harbours.
City where I live, not home, road that flowers with police,
what in all worlds am I doing here?

Morning in Madrid

Skirmish of wheels and bells and someone calling:
a donkey's bronchial greeting, groan and whistle,
the weeping factory sirens rising, falling.

Yelping of engines from the railyard drifted:
then, prelude to the gold-of-wine of morning,
the thunderstorm of iron shutters lifted.

The Café with the Blue Shrine

You push the soiled door-curtain back
and there, short-sighted, is the little café
garish and dirty in the city way;
like walls its very nature seems to peel and crack.

Sometimes a plucked string vivifies
that cave, and here the woman sang beside us
one of those Andalusian songs that touch
on tears, with . . . 'I am in love with you for your Moorish eyes . . .'

She had what offered for her stage,
where the blonde calendar pin-up with her smile
hung facing that blue shrine in which the Virgin
behind her Spanish iron-barred window like a cage

Inclined her crowned and childlike head
with mild uncomprehending country gaze:
these things seemed fitting. But one sombre listener
gaunt at his corner table, motionless as dead,

Black clothes, black beret, chin on hand,
alone, perhaps, heard that song down his bones;
and our eyes turned toward his speaking stillness
once more, when we had watched the knot of swaggerers stand

Dicing at the bar, the mirror flawed,
the squat black stove with curling python arm,
the girl's mouth shaking to that final blaze
of singing that we hammered on the tables to applaud.

Castanets

Back will go the head with the dark curls
and the foot will stamp:
but now she stoops beneath
her arms or, frowning, whirls
her skirt to lie out flat on the air
so the breeze is on
our mouths, and the smoke swings:
dry like a thirst the guitar rings.

Across her eyes drunk hair; the flower
that lodged there spins to the ground:
coolly in the barbarous dance
the wrists arch up, and now
the castanets, those fever teeth,
begin to sound:
then, gunshot through a veil,
blow the night suddenly mad with their pelting hail.

In Athens

Her hank and swing of hair
then – the whole face in a glance – the rounding line
of cheek, the childlike
mouth that is learning yet to be composed,
the chin, the joy of the neck; you know each feature
about this stranger
like things you have learned by finger-tips or drawing.

The knock inside your chest:
someone you loved was like her; there is given
neither name nor time, except it was long ago:
the scene, half caught, then blurred:
a village on the left perhaps, fields steeply rising.

A perturbation of pulse,
and a word your body is trying to make you hear
on a city corner. It is so much like
the twist in the plotting of things she should pass here
so near where they talked well on love
two civilizations ago, and found
splendid and jeering images: horses plunging,
that apple cut, the Hidden One.

                              A wryness,
and a name your body is trying to make you hear . . .

The Rendezvous

I take the twist-about, empty street
– balconies and drapes of shadow
– and glimpse chalk slogans on each wall,
(now governments have done their work)
that the fanatic or the duped,
even children are taught to scrawl:
the patriotic, 'Tyrants', 'Vengeance',
'Death to', etc.

                      Hooped
the barbed wire lies to left and right
since glass crashing, cars on fire,
since the mob howled loose that night,
gawky, rusty, useful wire
with little dirty fangs each way,
(what craftsman makes this fright?).
Black on that chemist's lighted window
steel helmets, rifle tops. I sense
the full moon wild upon my back
and count the weeks. Not long from this
the time we named comes round.

                    And true
to loves love never thought of, here
with bayonet and with tearing fence,
with cry of crowds and doors slammed to,
waits the once known and dear, once chosen
city of our rendezvous.

The Lottery Sellers

Beneath a gun grey sky
– with a wind savage out of Tartar places
– he barks four words to hurrying, lowered faces
and shakes his tickets with their potent numbers;
fluttering fortunes.

Gaze lifted over roof tops,
she calls four words in out-of-nowhere tones,
nailed as though cold could no more search her bones,
and droops her tickets lucky past all longings
or strength of stars.

Perhaps it will snow tonight:
two voices still keep with you as you go:
Luck never saw the sky hang charged with snow;
Wealth trembles, hugs his rag suit to his chest,
on a cold hell's corner.

Train to Work

9.20; the Underground groans him to his work;
he sits fumbling a letter; is that
a cheque attached? He is puzzled, frowns
sadly, like Rhesus monkeys, like us. Above
the frown fair hair is thinning. Specially
I celebrate his toes turned in, his worn
shoes splashed with mud (but his hands
are clean and fine), the bottoms of his striped trousers
crumpled by rain.
                              In a little while his station
will syphon him out with others, along, round, away
as a drop goes with its Niagara.
                              And because
he bears the cracking brunt of things he has never willed
and has eight mean hours a day
to live at the bidding of the gods, and is gentle and put upon,
this blindfold bull-fight nag, endearing stranger,
and before long, like others who come to mind,
is condemned to sure death, he sits
(with his mackintosh belt twisted),
poetry roaring from him like a furnace.

At 'The Angler'

The apple trees were all 'salaams' of clusters
in those walled gardens where the mown
grass, what with rains and years, took dents like peaches;
the bent old roofs, the trees, that grass
went on so with their lives there, we alone
seemed to be short of time to pass.

The world was summer and a doze, that pasturing
country so lazily inclined
down to the willow-wept, the swan-sailed river
and the eighteenth-century villages;
quelled river voices seeped the back of the mind
fooling the ear with distances.

And if rain rattled all night on the leaves,
the great night-crescent of the weir,
swollen with rainfall, growling its white tons
seemed to call pardon on our crime
of parting, cause more deep than now or here
talking to our short from its long time.

Lovers, we had our share of the ideal;
again, next day, with end of storm
how swans curved near as if to bring good omens
to us and – so love made it seem
there and then certain – in their trance of calm
blazed a white Always from that stream.

The Administrator

Some student I look after from this desk,
because of words I write down here,
grasps apparatus he had never known
or, weeks from home, speaking a foreigner's English,
spades English turf above a buried town.
He finds, but these words steer.

I flip back through the file, their photographs
talk out; a humorous Roman glance;
a German's, cunning spectacles, square head;
an Arab's passionate lip; and in a flash of
liking I stretch a point, cut back my dead
official cant. And chance

To look up from the page: one slow doom-burden,
storm vapours with torn fringes rolled
on Polar missions dark as they, the dour
rain ruled in slants on all things, start hard questions
on the humane, the human and on Power,
human to ask, but cold. But cold.

Night-time: Starting to Write

Over the mountains a plane bumbles in;
down in the city a watchman's iron-topped stick
bounces and rings on the pavement. Late returners
must be waiting now, by me unseen

To enter shadowed doorways. A dog's pitched
barking flakes and flakes away at the sky.
Sounds and night-sounds, no more; but then I catch
my lamp burn fiercer like a thing bewitched,

Table and chairs expectant like a play:
and – if that Unknown, Demon, what you will
stalks on the scene – must live with sounds and echoes,
be dammed the call to sleep, the needs of day,

Love a dark city; then for some bare bones
of motive, strange perhaps to beast or traveller,
with all I am and all that I have been
sweat the night into words, as who cracks stones.

Sud-Express

Our speed's perpetual howling like a strong wind
is a sudden snarl of lions as a bridge is torn by

    Fate does iron wedges drive

Objects silently collide; their sounds were somewhere dropped
leaving selected clatters, the booming voices behind me,
the plop of a cork, a fork tinkling, as heard through wool or water

    Going is a kind of treachery. I own it

Villages are caught asleep; they have no time to stir,
a man is lifting a latch, horse and harrow for ever
turn at the edge of a field, still as those fishermen
angling clouds and treetops along their shining river

    Even when I say 'I love you' it is tainted with goodbyes

We pelt the way we came with houses, saplings, flowers;
the middle fields swing, boil back and stream like lava;
forests of distance shake their necks and gallop with us.
Though the great wheel throws me southwards
keep those eyes for me still. If you can, love me

Boat Poem

I wish there were a touch of these boats about my life;
so to speak, a tarring,
the touch of inspired disorder and something more than that,
something more too
than the mobility of sails or a primitive bumpy engine,
under that tiny hot-house window,
which eats up oil and benzine perhaps
but will go on beating in spite of the many strains
not needing with luck to be repaired too often,
with luck lasting years piled on years.

There must be a kind of envy which brings me peering
and nosing at the boats along the island quay
either in the hot morning
with the lace-light shaking up against their hulls from the water,
or when their mast-tops
keep on drawing lines between stars.
(I do not speak here of the private yachts from the clubs
which stalk across the harbour like magnificent white cats
but sheer off and keep mostly to themselves.)

Look for example at the Bartolomé; a deck-full
of mineral water and bottles of beer in cases
and great booming barrels of wine from the mainland,
endearing trade;
and lengths of timber and iron rods for building
and, curiously a pig with flying ears
ramming a wet snout into whatever it explores.

Or the Virgen del Pilar, mantled and weavy with drooping nets
PM/708/3A
with starfish and pieces of cod drying on the wheel-house roof
some wine, the remains of supper on an enamel plate
and trousers and singlets 'passim';
both of these boats stinky and forgivable like some great men -
both needing paint,
but both, one observes, armoured far better than us against jolts
by a belt of old motor-tyres lobbed round their sides for buffers.

66

And having in their swerving planks and in the point of their bows
the never-enough-to-be-praised
authority of a great tradition, the sea-shape
simple and true like a vase,
something that stays too in the carved head of an eagle
or that white-eyed wooden hound crying up beneath the bowsprit.

Qualities clearly admirable. So is their response to occasion,
how they celebrate such times
and suddenly fountain with bunting and stand like ocean maypoles
on a Saint's Day when a gun bangs from the fortifications,
and an echo-gun throws a bang back
and all the old kitchen bells start hammering from the churches.

Admirable again
how one of them, perhaps tomorrow, will have gone with no hooting or
    fuss,
simply absent from its place among the others,
occupied, without self-importance, in the thousands-of-
millions-of sea.

Table-Tennis

Because the heavy lids will not drag up
I am playing table-tennis with eyes closed,
asleep, and striking at the sound;
with what a grovelling score may be supposed.

In my dream I am tired and long to stop.
Pit-ponies, sex-fiends, gypsies' bears have found
mercy, I hope, in sleep.

                      Each thump, each kick
or chastening of my day crowds back in this
unskilful ghostly tournament of poc-pic.

I know my Opponent; Who he is I miss.
The ordeal turns wilder than before;
now serve and smash must fly through a shut door.

The Leopards

One of them was licking the bars of its circus-cage
then gazing out sleepily round the tall tent splendid
just here and there with scarlet and brass,
till the bang of a whip

Brought the animals lolloping onto their chairs (a tail
hung long and twitching, talking its own thoughts.) Possibly
the threat was lies, it was not so much
the percussion

Of the whip, but instead some gipsy trick of the tents
won over these golden kittens to rise and beg
and flaunt their white, powder-puff bellies
(though at the report

Of a lash that curls too near, out flutters a paw
like a discharge from a fuse.)
                                        Now they were rolling
and cuddling with the bare-chest tamer;
now cowering at the whip-cut.

With humans one judges better; the tamed, the untamed.
It is harder with these pretenders – claws in, out,
– finally snaking off low to the ground:
yet there was a likeness, something stayed and haunted
as they bleared and snarled back over their narrow shoulders
at that whip banging.

A *Sunday*

A black Cordoba hat tilted
and the chin-strap
make it.

And she his white mare
with tail coiffured
coming in dancing
(her eyes of a tragedienne)
speak it.

Crowd-din like gravel falling;
an odour of expectation
and that odour

Which rounds her fastidious nostrils:
blood sweetening the air
of evening and October.

Cripples

On that kind island the brick-coloured earth
lavishes barley and pigtailed maize man-high;
olives lean heads together
(with the goat-flock under them some inkpot spills)
and half a mile of crack-car road will run
with surf of oleander flowers;
villas and farms are bleach and colour-of-sky,
and moderate, watered hills
spread harvests of grapes that the next hill will have outdone.

But fig and bean-trees bear such heavy crops
that out of age or wantoness of fruiting,
their branches give and sink
and farmers stick poles under them for props,
five or six to one fruiter's use;
so the trees stand when summer enters its height
(bolt-shot with perfume, leaf and juice)
like cripples on crutches or men crazed with drink,
staggering and laughing, arms hung up to the light.

Watchers

Their faces are untenanted. These were once,
and will again be so,
a village grandma with thin hair scratched back,
a ploughboy with spud nose and ragged mouth,
a father rigged for the town in his stiff black,
the brass stud at his lifted throat on show;
all tilted up one way
some of these faces keep half-smiles,
yet those smiles never grow.

Theirs are like faces sleep has drained. The dark
communion of dream which holds them world-aloof
is splashed with light from an arc. All their dear care
goes whispering and yearning
high above the sweep of circus benches
there where two manikins under the great bell-roof
walk down a hair;
he, prancing and masterful in his red-slashed shirt,
and slight and hesitant
she like a twist of paper turning.

The Wedding Pictures

Bulky with mackintosh and scarf
against the autumn weather
a man of pith and force, with grizzled hair
my friend the photographer

Brings me a sheaf of photos from the reception
for last week's wedding. There
exchanging gazes stand the couple together
under the Napoleon-period painting. Tall
or squat, caught out or posed, the guests parade,
myself among these categories somewhere;
there figure all
the smiles and all the hands that lift champagne
and – there was some joke then now past recall
– the bride again, pulling a comic face,
eyes wide and splendid.
                Why is it today,
with his hands full of gladness and beginnings
he comes reminding me of gnarled old truths,
staying to pass the gossip of his trade,
a trade that thrives wherever people gather;
new from his morning at the graveyard
and on his shoes the crust of graveyard clay?

73

By a Breakwater

At Dover the wind came spotting rain and whirled
gulls in big Catherine Wheels;
no holidaymakers dawdled on the front or neared the loud surf at all.

A storm-glare on that Castle, hung in the sky;
smoke downward streaking
from a ship heading East, and the sea out there with its snowing look.

I said there was no-one; a breakwater sheltered one couple
in their embrace tight-pulled,
they were plain, middle aged; with his right hand he was emptying

A hypodermic syringe in her bare arm
(I looked twice; fear of dreaming);
she leaned on him, quite reliant.
                                        It is to be remarked

This scene can be told for a laugh: at the hopelessness
of a summer; at the fantasy
of such an act and its setting; or at Medicine masked as Passion;

Also, for a shiver, the macabre.
                                        Or again, not squarely
for a joke or a flinching away
but, as here, for a sometimes blurred, other times emerging query,

Almost recognition. So clutched to each other, sitting nowhere
                                        and hiding from the wind.

Lop-sided

A pressure on the ears,
the explosion's stinging bang
jammed with that blinding nerve of flame torn down,
the houses jumping dark
rain grossly hose-ing;
rivers heading eagerly down the street hub-level
colliding at corners, trying to climb back into fountains,
revolving rubbish.

We had remarked few warning preliminaries,
having the day to get through, that's how it is;
lassitude indeed, and yawning, something strange in the movements
of insects or birds:
nothing to end up this way.

Not consciously
had we been aware of such massive disproportions accumulating
quietly and long,
calling for that smashing and flying of space-architecture,
globe-scale outrage,
august grievances to be dreadfully righted,
leaving a sniff of burning.

Donkey

He belongs under a blow-torch sky
as much as selling water, or carrying beds through the street
or endlessly standing around;
he with big dirty hearthrug head and gorgeous eye,
he with his stripe of vigour, who raging in the heat
and belly-ache of love throws bitter complaint out with the sound
of croup, of cars braking, of hinges, a last-ditch cry.

Ankling along the cobbles of a cliffside, breakneck street
or the tracks of the bald plains or spinbrain mountain-twists,
he has come to a peace with servitude and those by whom he is downed;
let us waive further pathos, as he would;
for him there is no defeat:
turds entice him, but mostly he dreams straight on (and his ankles
    are tiny like children's wrists).

Hung with cheap lines of pottery,
bashed milk-cans, brushes, prayer-rugs or kindly wood,
taken for granted, loved or merely used,
with the master piled amid,
he props the four-hooved beast-and-human pyramid
that though stone yielded has withstood,
and points up over the early bones,
relic and monument . . .
donkey on business, treading the weeds past side-pitched pillar-drums
– pillars of the lost, imperial, the earthquake-tumbled towns.

Full Moon

Doubtful-edged and almost daylight
on marbles and the blank page of white walls;
drooping the little flowered tree
along my street in Chinese-paintbrush falls;

Mocking unfootfalled streets with moonshine,
moonlight rubs meaning as the sea rubs stones;
and does Time's sum again; tonight is
tonight and the last moon that disturbed my bones.

Close the sun-torn shutters, step
back to the lampbulbs' poor barn-theatre glow
or the prisms and rage of Southern noon,
and grieve and laugh in roles you too well know:

snow-crater light will prove how false they show.

The Agents

Anywhere your agents search me out:
in stations at night as I am going from where
you are not to where you are not,
thinking of God knows what under all stars,
in that shouting twilight
a stranger hurries, intent like others; there
my body alerts as when a danger jars.

In a bank they walk, or instantly torn
past me in cars; or as a child some days;
a week ago on those stone
stairs winding up to my work – the identical
managing of a scarf;
or some old letter dropped about displays
your fierce script like glass jags that top a wall.

Let them keep startling as before,
frequenters of half-lights, the improbable;
they have been my friends for
such long and earthquake years.
                                    Do not now state
they have not your orders,
anyhow that you do not wish them well,
while you sit proud, in the North, and hug your hate.

Chestnuts

First the demure green handkerchiefs let droop,
(what comedy was I up to then?)
next, one remembers almost to the day,
all that short brilliance of stuck birthday-lights
that brought the summer forward in a bound
(did pleasures or the rough deals get their way?)

Now in this lane where otherwise you listen
to a distant tractor and harrow working round
– which you can't glimpse; the weeds wave up such heights
– slither and run,
falling through parched leaves like the tearing of paper,
the conker thumps down, bursts its capsule wide
and rolls haphazard to its rest,
grandly prolific, in the wheel-marked dust;
first time in the light (and meaning my goodbye;
I know, I will not delay)
conker with a piece of the sun
of a flaring autumn on one waxy side.

Blue Arm

A high pink wall; plaster in map shapes peeling;
socks on the dangle; a row of windows; and over
the pots of flowers a blue arm reaches out, feeling.

Into a courtyard white-collared children are turning;
talking hums up in light like days at the seaside,
sound is the sun-daze, voices fuse in a burning.

And it all is an answer, perhaps; last night, unsleeping
I fought with a problem of writing; how to liberate
a certain thought into words, its own and leaping
(comfortless X-ray bones, the hours crept weeping).

Perhaps I shall find out how. Above the laughing
animation the blue arm pushes a window; sunstabs
are shaken my way over tree-tops. Heliographing.

Near Aranjuez

Ungated fields of yellowish earth
that chalk and flint peer through:
alone on the left hand hill a whitewashed chapel
with four dark trees, like stilted, elegant birds:
presently a crumbling tower; there was once
something forgotten now to love, to guard.

Coral is not more gradual than that castle
becomes gold debris, loosening stone from stone:
past sixty windy miles the April mountains
slowly unwinter; plaid cape to his chin
a peasant eyes us as he rides
with bundled firewood down a dust-plumed road
the Roman vanguards found.

On the Road

Our roof was grapes and the broad hands of the vine
as we two drank in the vine-chinky shade
of harvest France;
and wherever the white road led we could not care,
it had brought us there
to the arbour built on a valley side where time,
if time any more existed, was that river
of so profound a current, it at once
both flowed and stayed.

We two. And nothing in the whole world was lacking.
It is later one realizes. I forget
the exact year or what we said. But the place
for a lifetime glows with noon. There are the rustic
table and the benches set; beyond the river
forests as soft as fallen clouds, and in
our wine and eyes I remember other noons.
It is a lot to say, nothing was lacking;
river, sun and leaves, and I am making
words to say 'grapes' and 'her skin'.

COLLECTED POEMS, 1965

The Empire Clock

Muted wood-wind is one noise of the traffic, and there is a second
when trams manoeuvre the bend, the muffled grinding and wail
of steel turned on steel.

The River drifts its ice under no stars towards
the Black Sea (and what winter cities?). The long-silent
Empire clock with its pediment

Abruptly intones once. Rather than a chime, a stirring,
a gruffness. And instantly I am conscious of the young man
from the war in nineteen-fifteen

Who cut on the back door in this house his 'goodbye'
to his girl, and the date.
                                    Fifty-odd winters it stayed, that thought,

Which we painted out. Which we painted out.

On the 'Sievering' Tram

Square figures climb off and on;
mufflers, Astrakhan hats.
A wintry night for a ride to a clinic
to visit a new-born boy and his mother;
and the bell hurrah-ing.

Too many life-bullied faces
packed on the Sievering tram.
Yet a woman smiles at a baby near her
and beckons and beckons, as we run lurch
-ing, and sigh and restart.

That baby views the woman steadily;
(and the floor is all mucked with snow.)
What do I bring to the boy and his mother
lying in the clinic? Daffodils,
bewilderment and love,

Ready money, a clock and a signature.
A Neon-light Pegasus glows in the sky
(Somebody's Oil) as we swing corners
past bakers' and laundries and snow, with the traffic
-gongs ringing like glory.

The Invaders

They would bar your way in the street
to grab your astounding watch;
that unknown thing, a handkerchief,
they would threaten you for, and snatch
to enrich a village wife
a hemisphere far off;
a firearm gave them right.

Girls wore soiled, frumpy clothes,
scrubbed make-up away, looked rough
when they hurried down to the shops;
that was the epoch's vogue.

Through a longing to look older
one woman put powder on her hair
– well-worn Occupation stories;
there is this which a few prefer:

The child asking for a tame rabbit;
some kindly foreigners who heard;
and her cry and her flight from the soldier bringing
seven dead rabbits with blood
on their fur, and their necks swinging.

A Number

Looking up from her knitting, Anne said 'Fifty three';
the number of stitches along her needle?
It could be the number of a wintry tram behind the house
whistling and howling across the meat-freezing bridge,
or digits of a crucial telephone number
or a friend's street door in London or in Vienna;
it might have been something of moment that took place in the year
one thousand nine hundred and fifty three, before
we raised those first drinks to each other in Gran Via, Madrid.

Knitting, she called to mind the women
knitting shawls by the scaffold in the French Revolution
– there were probably young faces seen there.
She reminded me also of the Fates at their woolly occupations.
'Was it the stitches?'
                                'No, today is your birthday.'
                                                                Naturally
I had forgotten my birthday, and my age as fifty three.
'I thought you meant the stitches in the row.'
I said 'Count them'; she counted. The number was fifty three.

When she visited a clinic, later, her room was Fifty Three.

Properties of Snow

Snow on pine gorges can burn blue like Persian
cats; falling on passers can tip them with the eloquent hair
of dancers or Shakespeare actors;
on roads can mute the marching of a company of infantry
(so that they seem the killed from a battle whispering by);
neglected, glues where you walk, a slippery black iron,
famous hospital-filler,
proved friend of bandages and white hip-length plaster.
Decorative and suspicious: wine broken recently on snow . . .
Spaded with tinkles and grating
from a pavement, presently huddles in a heap blotched and disgraced,
a pedigree pet, now repellent.

On office, on factory roofs,
or stretching, severe, to horizons on trees, fields, fences,
with no way across except the way the traveller will plough;
nothing moving, and a sky the colour of grey trousers;
blanched snow, the Chinese colour of mourning, of death,
can rob the bones of their marrow,
turn a man's face towards home.

Clemente

The pride of Clemente was that the drinks he brought were fiercer
than those of Manolo, Rafael or Ventura, waiters at the Club;
he would linger and smile,
and watch you taste those drinks. (Clemente, and wouldn't you watch?)

Clemente died. One imagines strangers at the funeral, and foreigners,
bizarre, beside his family. He must have been very much mourned,
that man must have been,
by many who could never properly have known him, or dreamed his
   thoughts

When he went off duty. Kindness, a look in the eyes, a few stories;
what does it mean, to be 'known'?

               Abroad, I dwell on his boast,
(whatever text was cut into his headstone)
echoing so strange in death, yet holding to its old grandeur:
'Clemente who wangles you the cruel drinks.'

You

Subways have similar gunbarrel perspectives
to those which, furlong laid
after furlong, you now thread.
If there were a friend
he might take the next man for you, or the one preceding
with his regular tread.
Aloft and on each side
hands and fingers are staring at you,
whose vigilance you will not evade.

Tonight you swing past odours of cattle, the breath of grass;
then colder smells, brine and decaying sea-plant;
a star trails with you half your course.

Always, voyaging or clambering the rocks of the further bay,
such is your infirmity
that your words have to be spoken for you by others,
and perhaps in a different country.
                              You on the way
The name of which appalls,
from the hope-withering corridors on the mainland
to the treeless island pinnacled with the never-broken walls.

Dr Karl Lueger

Frock-coated Dr Karl Lueger
– bronze hand to bronze heart –
on his plinth in front of the cafés
where the morning shoppers sit
has exchanged his snow-tippet
and his middle European
busby of snow
for ribbons and runnels of pigeon-shit.

On the road below where the Doctor stands
I am watching a sparrow entirely absorbed
in eating a crust without help of hands.
With so much whip and flap
either the crust or the head
or both will be landing on someone's lap.

To Piers Spencer, five months old

You form and feel words over on your lips
mutely; for you words still are shapes of mouths.

If you become a poet, and short of pence
(your father's son even in this plight),
you will also mumble away, and citizens,
whose own words tumble out, and never a hitch,
will cower, when you compose, in fright.

Though others you will find throw looks of greed;
less daunted by your mimic speech:
So much your fellow-human-beings they are,
they will edge your way, and speculate
how if they could get closer somehow and overhear,
they might learn something that would make them rich.

Traffic in April

Returning West from our visit to the Embassy
– with four files on my knee – the car turned right;
there was chaos, then; we needed at once to turn left
but cars from that street were swinging (their left) across us;
and cars from opposite advanced; there were neither lights nor
    policeman.
A car nosed forward, clinched the jam. The Austrian
driver lifted his hands from the wheel and sat guffawing.
All those cars hooted; it was April, the snow just melted,
stone angels on roofs in sunlight, and the church towers;
the golden hands of the clocks glittering.

A quarter of a mile further a car fled by at fifty;
its front axle broke; it tilted, tore the road up,
continued, tried to bury itself in the road.
No-one was hurt; that axle glowed with the glow
of furnace steel spilling from a great spoon in a factory.
It was sunset and lightning together; the road burned,
the axle burned. We had little
German or English for communication,
but the two of us, clambering out to gawp,
on that fine particular day
had the kind of language needed for a screw-loose world, and for
    laughing.

Most things having a market price
My ears are full of the buzzing of the price.
Money dances in front of the page. I rise
And go to live as my money buys.

I've food to suffice. But out of day
Height doom and delight are narrowed away;
Anxiety takes what I wish to say;
Invention winters a worm's way.

I, Jack, walking on the hill's shoulder
Arm me to me, prevent myself becoming
Barky trees becoming earth that earth
Today hard under my heel as a boulder,
Forged with frost: trees that soon a bolder
Month will send fountaining with leaf, earth
The crops are going to crumble and dance through. Hold
Myself as man from re-earthing, the drift to be homing.
I having to remember who I am when I am. Hang
To friends scattered across England; but having
To remember how long there is to remember; long
To be living when there is place, not difference and wring;
But having in a given time to hunt like gold
This: the singly achieving some thing.

The Runner

As a trained racket hand's sweep
As breasting air a swallow-diver's
Liquid fall; straight straight homing
No other boy can pace him, he is a greyhound, makes them creep
Laughing out for him is another act of running.

Wounds like raw iron fed to the wheel,
The people's drugged sense of injury,
If these must grind, then thrust out killing edge;
Feet hungry for ground, lounging ignorant good will
Can stay loved, no straws be drawn, have a neutral's privilege.

Winter Landscape

The spiky distance was the town; spires,
Factories, gasworks, shrunken in the telescope of blue.
If there was any sound
Across that giant nerveless palm of ground
– Work from the rail – its action was long done,
And it came limping late on lame feet
Past the tiny horses among the steel floods.
Brush over the sky with endless weeping clouds
Ascending towards us from those thorns; the town.

Near the bridge an aeroplane was perched.
I saw the pilot square in his padded coat
Smoking, chatting to friends.
He mounted, waved to the three waving friends;
Turned the plane, jolting, on to even ground:
Then she ran up wind with an excitement of engines,
Poised her bird's tail, was in air now, sweeped about
As a sower throws, a waker stretches, and
Strong up some sky-scent followed, glad as a hound.

The House

There that terrible house, those corridors
Fluffed with sound-proof material
Where a glove is drawn over feel of good and evil:
And men move whom wages move, but without belief.

Wages and hum-drum made the thin, forbidden,
Mouth of this young girl. She admires a man
Who has not seen her. How she smiles at her hands
In secret, as if sharing a joke with someone.

A simpleton claws at money across my mind.
A speed-king hunches in his cockpit. Lovers
Go spry to the pictures – it is Saturday. Marchers
Sing, furrow the fountained square: Whom fanaticism,

Hunger, hunted; speed to crumple distance
Or any lust electrified to burst bound
From that terrible house; them I stand with outside.
That house I know: I live now: therefore love them.

Going to the Country

Now ranging cracker-brilliant areas
Where the higgledy shops shout each other down
And cinemas carved as mosques sell to the humbled
An evening as the hero who breaks all bars,
Our bus rolled towards country wood and down:
Now less lighted stretches; residences whose
Stony outside – porches for knees, severe
Shuttered windows under eyebrows of stone
Suggested councillors, business men of mark,
Or seated Egyptian dead. Through these we were
A horn of light butting through straits of twilight . . .
Now wealth, now the market. At last, open and dear
To drivers a world made simply of road, and stark,
Where sky and earth were one coalmine of dark.
Fingers jabbed North and to the coastal towns.
In Town we had many friends, and of confidence,
Who didn't need us to reckon or be stilted,
Good company at drinks, enquiring and witty
At the play or in the street. They would have lent their sense
To explore or ignore a public life disordered
As a photograph from a war with a steeple tilted.
They would be up. Country was early to bed.
But far from them, with colder air to breathe,
Lying under a country roof we are content
To hear – we would have given each other voice
– One trudging step which crossed the yard beneath:
And because nothing else moved, that one noise spread
At least to the cirrus cloudlets overhead,
That top of ceilings. We were pleased with our choice.

Picked Clean from the World

Picked clean from the world by the speed of our train
We lay the uneasy night
Seeming to lurch through cloud
To drop like an aerial jumper
To explore at random the cisterns of the rain
The deafening workshops of the thunder.

In the morning, the sunny plateaux, shrubs
That claw up fierce from an earth baked dry
And writhe black arms like a fire's stubs,
Feathered olives, and the lolling maize
Dangling its carter's whips,
And the vine, knee-high.

To enter alertly a new town-square,
To cross the equator of shade and glare,
To smell and touch snow;
New adjustments to a new life shaped
By female harbour or river's flow
– Mind needed these as body bread.
At home, in an industrialized country
No other wish will do instead
Of that ancient disruptive wish, springing naked
Like a dream whose sense we are made to know.

Just as at Pont du Gard
Where the river is broad across the gravel,
Grateful because of the shade, and level,
Bathers who look up are
Hit with astonishment,
Seeing suddenly the Roman viaduct,
Its trampling arches of yellow stone,
With its stilted valley-stride
Fill all the sky one way,
Enduring and monstrous in its image of travel.

They Tell a Lie

Parted, the young and amorous touch tragic hands by letter.
The world between is a factory of fear. It is thought better
    Not to admit why.

Active men are chucked like slag to waste or at length
Given such work they can use the mere half of their strength;
    It is dangerous to ask why.

Many died spilt from air, in deserts or in the sea's
Murdering lanes, or boxed in the trap of cellars. These
    Should not have been told a lie.

I walk between walls of war and mark in a gesture or an eye
Sure as alkali and acid, those who would deeply deny
    What we are fighting for and why.

The weather beats and blows, and the scene will not keep still
And some must die but the water has got to go down the hill,
    Though today they tell a lie.

In Memoriam

The earth slumped in
and through successive empires those two stayed,
tomb-thieves, splendid beyond their title, free
of a King's palace. Round the walls there swayed
forms of beast-cowled, bird-pinioned deity;
corn in a precious bin
stood there with wine beside the treasure load
to tend the Soul on its tremendous ways
and from a nearness still uncrossed-to glowed
long buried Pharaoh's visored golden gaze.
Scholars, the second stir
since that first burial year
found them where the earth held them in its cramps,
finger-bones hooked to Alexandrian lamps.

The ciné-camera pointed
and the tall hatted Frenchman stands through Time
next to the boulevard 'pissoir' he has left
buttoning his trousers. Anger starts to climb
into his face. Outmoded passers, reft
decades from their appointed
age, throw a glance or pause to stare our way;
dead eyes alive from a dead Paris day.

By the cold church wall
stern on their knees the Tudor couple pray
starched into wood with those great ruffs they wore
and in descending scale of small array
sharp upward handed all their family score.
If we ask at all
impertinent questions of their loves and fears
or when they smiled, be certain this is how
they would face Time. Some gold and red adheres
upon their angular draperies even now
once from the wet brush new.
Both as mortals dead
and honoured, haughty red
and gold their burial due.

The Top-Storey Room

Above London sailed my room
with clouds and evenings.
Tidied from day to day
by the woman with the low voice and the sad mouth,
its emptiness assumed my character
and watched me like my portrait.

To blind my room
I lived the disorder of London
hoping that in some bar or entrance-way
among the years of brick
a face would suddenly flare into the truth;
but there were only the faces.
     Then at night
it was good to unlock my room, to find
my papers, the cheap desk, my books
waiting by the bed.

     Yet sometimes
potent with memory, on the morrow of storms,
mornings grew wings, the seagulls came
blown across dreamed of waves and miles to visit
the flagposts, or to wheel
across my window pane, and dazzle
the air like juggler's knives.

Four Translations
(from the Italian of Eugenio Montale)

The Lemon Trees

Listen, the poet laureates
move only among plants with unfamiliar names:
box or acanthus.
For me, I love the roads which find their way to grassy
ditches where in half dried pools the boys
catch a few famished eels;
the tracks which follow the slopes
descend between tufts of reeds
and end in the back gardens among the lemon trees.

Better if the clamour of the birds
vanishes swallowed in the sky:
clearer sounds the murmur
of the friendly branches in air that hardly moves
and the touch of this smell
which never quite leaves the earth
and fills the heart with a restless languor.
Here like a miracle the war
of the torn passions is silent
here to us poor falls our share too of riches,
the smell of the lemons.

See, in these silences when things
yield themselves and seem about to betray
their ultimate secret
sometimes the feeling comes
of discovering a flaw in Nature,
the dead point of the world, the link that does not hold
the thread to unravel which finally lands us
in the centre of a truth.
The eyes fumble round
the mind searches, tunes, parts asunder
in the scent which spreads like a stain
when the day gradually tires.

The silences in which one sees
in every human shadow that draws away
some disturbed divinity.

But the illusion fails and time brings us back
into loud cities where the blue shows
only in scraps high up between the eaves.
Rain tires the earth; the tedium
of winter thickens on the houses,
light becomes a miser – the soul bitter.
When one day through a half-closed doorway
among the trees in a courtyard
shines out the yellow of the lemons;
and the ice of the heart melts
and in our breasts peal
their songs
the golden trumpets of sunlight.

Don't ask us for the word which cuts and shapes
our formless spirit, there are letters of flame
to utter, nothing to shine like a crocus
lost in the middle of a dusty field.

Fortunate he who walks serenely
on good terms with himself and others,
indifferent to his shadow the glare of summer
prints on a flaking wall!

Don't ask us the formula to lay worlds open,
there is only some twisted syllable dry like a twig.
Only this today we can tell you,
the thing we are not, the thing we do not want.

Bring me the sunflower so that I can transplant it
into my soil burnt with brine,
for it to show all day to the sky's mirroring blue
the anxiety of its amber face.

Things that are dark lean towards clarity
the bodies of things flow out and empty themselves
in colours: colours in music. Vanishing
is therefore the luckiest of chances.

Bring me the flower which leads
to the springs of transparent gold
where life like an essence turns to vapour
bring me the sunflower crazed with light.

To shelter, pale and preoccupied
in the shadow of a burning garden wall,
to listen among the plum trees and ivy tendrils
to the clucking of thrushes, the rustling of snakes.

In cracks of the ground or on the vetch
to watch the files of red ants
now breaking, now entwining
from the tops of tiny hillocks.

To watch between leaves the far-off
pulsing of the spangled sea
while a tremulous shrilling of cicada
rises from the bald peaks.

And walking in the sun which dazzles
to feel with wonder and sadness
how all life and its pain
is in this following a wall
crowned with sharp splinters of bottle.

Pino

Pino, a hill top village, slanting street
and at the corner a wall where gossips sit
in a row at sunset, like migrating birds,
backed by the sky and forty miles of plain.

Buses heading for somewhere else; the words
cart wheels grind and jerk or a peasant cries
as the white oxen lift their swinging throats,
somnambulists with long Egyptian eyes.

The 'National' inn, the sleepy, smiling maid,
the queenly, fat Madame in a dress of spots;
simple kindnesses like that harsh strong wine;
and two weeks blank of great events. In fine

A time of waiting. Most of our life is that.
But waiting sometimes vivid with the sign
of things amazingly connected; whether some
day of thunder or night with the Plough slung over
the road to the towns and what there was to come.

Casa de P_____.

The bell and parade of winking girls,
the writhing and the shrinking from foot to foot
were invented by Harry the American who cheats
the world in rice from a seat at the Palace Bar.
That evening was created from our guts,
the allurements, the suggestion of disinfectant,
from things we had dreamed, feared, wanted; there were many
threw slivers in the cauldron that it steamed from.
That frowning man-at-arms, the enormous bawd
brown-jumper-armed, was made by my headmaster:
the Puritan one who died of drink, whose sex-talks
each red-faced boy was sworn to silence over:
he was the avenging nightmare of those warnings.
Fitz invented the room hung full of knickers
and invented the whore waiting for her client
reading *La Mujer Vencida* (paper covers).
The prints in this stained hall, of classical scenes –
rotund limbs of muses, shaded columns –
were my art mistress? Who robbed the life from
the Red Indians that we drew. Where is she now?
Someone, perhaps a rich invalid at Worthing,
imagined the elderly, aproned serving-woman
whose hopeless, tired eyes stare through this poem.
    It is clear, of course, the evening never existed,
and what seemed flesh – that blonde, the gleaming Arab,
were dust or grass or mere hallucination,
for which in a way we were all responsible,
and a gossiping Protestant clergyman from Athens
seemed to descend with us the ill-lighted stair
stone by stone with all their doubts and turnings
to the watchman fumbling keys in the empty street
and all that the moon regarded with such eyes.

The Clock

When the great convent clock strikes
up there from its facing tower
there is no shield between us, and the swell
enters my house like a wave and my rooms are bell.

I wonder what chimes mean to those
wing-hatted hidden nuns,
(linen and wood and nails); the rolling;
quarter to the hour; the hour. The planets tolling.

And I tangle out with the back of my mind
– looking across the deserted
walks and the low long roofs of their entombing
– my own reflective affection for that booming.

Which is that is grimly faithful,
that lead and iron friend,
and lends a touch of theatre or of rhyme;
one is Prince today and Clown the other time.

Yet, joke of fate to send me here
in sound of such a watchman;
the hour is ill although the night be prime
for me who abhor a watch through dread of Time!

I, wishing, hating refugee
from Time, who love his medium:
and at my hand, as that wry voice discloses
Time's creature too, this brimming wine, these globed
    and lolling roses.

For Signorina Brunella Mori

Tell me, you Romans, who but the dark Brunella,
    giovane, bella,
could ever give such a startling twist to the hoary
    'memento mori'?

A *Ward*

A ward dim like a wagon-lit; quick footsteps,
commotion of whispers; one bed curtain-bright;
shadows of the doctors bowing and straightening,
small, huge; small, huge. Methylated-ether tang.

Next day the air still keeps its eyes averted
when he has gone, with the gentle
rumble and clink of wheels. All fitting comment
seems to have crept away, too.

Young nurses tiptoed pulling curtains round
along the way he took, a decency
(if for our sakes, not his)
for which we are grateful. Blinding us was human.

Whatever knowledge we are capable of,
on a reckoning it will take a little while
of the kind, brisk, brittle hospital routine
to numb a memory, perhaps of only
a head drawing hard breath still, tipped back, eyes closed, chin fallen,
an arm flung from the sheets;

Or thoroughly needed to cleanse
this new taint of our general heritage
from a shining ward that neighbours
well-built Knightsbridge and lordly Hyde Park Corner.

Black Cat

Black cat
sleepily narrowing his eyes at me,
putting up a thick tail like smoke from a steamer,
speaking in a small rusty voice;
then trotting ahead, making short
friendly runs half sideways;

Cat in a garden of tawny and crimson
great still unfolding roses;
lawns smudgy underfoot after the downpours,
air tangy, bonfire raging,

Cat in a garden with roses in the September evening,
birds alert on the trees, worms like corkscrews sprouting,
fish in the pond plopping rings;

Myself thinking through roses, Autumn, pools and fire,
at the end of an episode in my life,
on the edge of a journey,
the auguries good;

And circling out from these paths paced along
tomorrow's or next year's passions, railroads, gardens . . .
and – with dear famous promises, and lies
– mountains, amazements, what new cities rumour.

Castille

Smouldering moon and stars like flaming crosses,
midnight the hour,
Spain; lovers walking past my balcony
and the clock banging out from the convent's pointed tower.

I sense the historic plain, the olive orchards,
and whatever it is that tries
past roofs and starlight to be understood,
as the answer tries to speak from a peasant's or a statue's eyes.

Such nights or noons I start to know this people,
how within they carry the sear
of Summer and blizzard and the short brash Spring,
gaunt valleys with the crash of water falling sheer;

Now all their gentleness must root in soil
sterner than ours:
boulder and scrub and mountains shaped like pain;
hearts that ferment with gold and dust, dead bones and crowns and
    flowers.

This Day

Though passion for her is my life's mere commons
some days, and this, stand clear – but the rendezvous,
the impersonal, busy bar, the City morning,
her books, her voice, were only those I knew.

There have been so many days, so many rooms:
yet from that very noon with the light streamed in
around the curtain's edge, and the darkened bed,
after two years I drink her breath, her skin.

Witness

You play the tape-recorder back;
there is yesterday again and the known and urgent voices;
there too (it was never in your yesterday)
is the gear-clash of a lorry moving up towards the mountains.
Paper chattering,
a bell ringing, a door that bangs,
a clack of glass on a table come shouldering among your voices.

You handle photos taken at a party;
exquisite and impertinent among the faces triumph
intruders you never noticed: electric fittings,
the grin of a useful ashtray, the splashy veining on marble.
An irruption?
What in the name of all that is Thing-born
did you expect? You were genial or fervent; and there was present,

Loyal to its loyalties, that Box
with the mad face and the whirling features to eat and spue you;
or when there were Lais, da Vinci and Socrates,
Byron and Catherine of Russia at your humdinger party,
then
all goggles and windows like a fly
the camera, soapy and cold to the holding fingers, blinked at it.

Written on a Cigarette Packet

Bloody lonely without you.
                              Stilettos;
your light voice locked in the tape-recorder,
                                        batteries run down.
Rum-drumming of motor-bikes
and under the arc of Jupiter
the summer-night balconies talking to each other
and the bar 'El Tenis'
                      to the bar 'Juan'.

That cloth folded on the radio is probably
folded just as you left it folded.
(Jupiter South-East about its purposes)
Perhaps I am also away;
my jacket I tossed across that chair
seems to have a ghost recumbent inside it.
'Stiletos'. You wrestle with Spelling.
                                  'Stiletoes'.

Jupiter topple to blazes;
                      for lack of you
I stare at your card propped on the mantelpiece
with your spelling, 'Stilletos'.

From the Military Academy

At evening from the Military Academy
bugles blow up red clouds west of my apartment,
bugles with the bell-notes and the
tingling ones blow white stars
up, the big first kind;
nail gold leaf on skyscraper windows
Eastward; and citizens
at the hour of bugles rumble their shutters up
and dogs bark, nervous.

And because these bugles fidget for attention
to matters in the past or hazards of sometime
(it seems the future),
but with imprecise meaning,
I write about bugles to be hell-rid of the
worry and recurrent itch of bugles
when corners of the streets belong to the young,
boys and girls who join them,
creatures of an early noon.

The Train Window

Stroked like a reflection high up on the train window,
an apparent trick of sight, they haunt up into
snow-mountain tops right above you hours away,
hazed, with a wet flash of the sun on them
and, lower, a faint hatching
of rock-strata;
                         they wear the authority of
all-there-is-to-be-said about a problem, or
are like something you wanted to make.
                              Are also
what you need presently to turn your eyes from.
Whatever it is up there, extreme to endure,
you encounter enough of it
in the look of that torrent, down on the level
on which we say goodbye to someone, or return to her:
its darkness racing the train wheels,
bare branches of winter saplings reaching over it,
and its white foam-bursts tumbling over backwards.

OXFORD POEMS

The lights with big elegant fingers
moulded and twined together and parted
the dancers' pliant bodies of pink plasticine:
the slim young man was whipped by the music like
      a top round the stage,
    ringing the cymbals with each kick of his feet.
but when the music was water rising in a lock
   you entered buoyed on the froth of the chorus' dancing
      whose smiles you alone could unstick.
  you alone the perched electrician in the wings
    forgot to hold caught in the net of his lantern
      and slid to his desire down the plank of the light.
for you alone above the plump knees of the chorus
the spirit of the audience stretched from the velvet tiers
  pursuing round the stage your elusive limbs
with tenuous arms of tobacco smoke.

          [*Sir Galahad*, vol. I, no. 1 (29 Feb. 1929), p. 31]

Schedules

The urgent ringing of the electric alarum
    brought forth a Spring of gold station masters;
out came the waistcoated porters like bees;
    the telegraph posts had passed down the word,
and the signals on their stilts had seen it a long way off
    the soundless threading of the smoke,
as if a burning finger were drawn through the landscape,
    and they stood waving their arms in excited semaphore;
the clock, an experienced patron of sport,
    with the face of a judge ticked out the seconds;
and the people tinkling pennies at the slot machines
    seemed to be taking bets with robot bookies;
now the tremors of the sound coming
    made ripples on the sea of cloth caps and bowlers;
up and down went officials stemming the overflow;
    the bosomed woman sprouted hands
multitudinous as an Indian goddess,
    and in every hand was a child;
each man clutched his prospects, his future,
    packed up in his handbag;
each man for himself!
    the last bend was turned;
round went the faces like blown leaves on a tree
    and in came the train
chasing the expectation of itself,
    sweating and panting,
wiping its face with a large white pocket handkerchief.

[*Sir Galahad*. vol. I, no. 2 (May 14, 1929), p. 19]

Festa

Because it was the Queen's birthday
we had all run up our spirits' pennons to the top of
    our flagposts
and skimmed about on the surface of our lives
like little flies on water:
No-one knew what to do
but they were all sure they were doing it:
the motor-bicycles went round in circles
arguing at the tops of their voices,
and the clapping started up
and tried to drown them
with a thousand clattering cylinders:
the slim young jockeys
balanced on the handlebars
and they and the paper hats and painted bladders
chased each other in and out through the forest of the smoke.

The mouth-organ man
with his shoulders over his ears
    rhapsodized.
'Grass all over our trousers,
    patterns of grass on our hands
our pleasure crowns the day's gold cornet
    and fills the embrace of our demands.'
'Fête champêtre by the marquees:
    the only death O Lord
is when the roundabout leaves the ground,
    the halfpenny leaves the board.'

Then they cleared away the sun
and up went the fire balloons
carrying with them the burning by which they climbed
enthusiasms cut loose
never looking down
till the fire went out from under them
and left them lying about all over the sky.

The rockets said 'Ah!'
leaping like gold fish
from a white splash of upturned faces
and arched their swan necks
to join point to point
in a suspended electrical kiss;
their broken passion sparkled down the sky
like downward champagne bubbles.
    But the continuous roundabout music
which was the engine that drove the day's excitement
stopped: and the fiery porcupines
pursuing each other nose to tail in mid air
stopped: and our spirits' last rockets were fired
and our eyes full of ashes:
    and the moon came up
to sweep away the crowds and the rocket smoke
with a mind soured like a domestic servant's
who only sees the morning's broken bottles and dirty glasses.

[*Oxford Poetry* 1929), pp. 46–47]

After Love

His absentness, his evading
Of her fierce identifying love
Was not self-prisoner's,
Marked him rather as one

When the fire fell who gave
Self as a thing most precious.
This the worse lover
In giving but counting . . .

At rare after-meetings
Now is the disappointed,
Wounded with self given,
Apartness once given.

Her easy talking, quick
Child's confidences, the cool
Hand given make irony
Of the natural images

He had matched her with – of birds
For her changing moods, new trees
And all swift creatures' kind
For her body.

Of Nature so, who drew
Her blood from Earth's heart, gave
Love unreflectingly,
She, changed so easily.

Wondered, is again natural,
By the young of animals
Is imaged, whose eyes forget
Late pain, by this hour's

Young sky new out of clouds
Printless of all Time's past.

[*Oxford Poetry* (1931), pp. 34–35]

125

Poem

After the wheels and wings of this intense day
Evening makes the sky big; as harvest's end
Final, the fields of strong hands empties.

In day, in the tide's, in the great flame's reaching
My hard want of you would have been easier to bear
Companied by men's and creatures' need, roots' thirst.

The hour that unstrings the world, horizons tilting
Blind into dark, earth undressed of life,
Stone, moon, point moving on sky map,

Holds all bitterness, littles the will so imperious,
Shows to will's self its dream-weak feet and hands, giant
That clock and sheer machine by which it starves.

[*Oxford Poetry* (1931), p. 36]

126

Clouded, Still, Evening

Breathing in leaf only
And in quick stem earth lies.
Known hills and the first star
Day's hot breath misted out.

Eyes left from need's service
See world too enfranchised;
Fearfully hands touch
Grass, trees, strange, not ours.

Men's ways in this silence
Seem far, and men's business;
Fine sense thought-distance sent
To left and right reports

Dominion of blind hills
And a world of close leaves.

Though I feel each tree's burden,
Earth's sap and strength,
To my pride and my doubting
I know no echo here,

By sympathy too exiled:
To this dark state, my source,
As man not native, even
Among men's corn stranger.

[*Oxford Poetry* (1931), p. 37]

127

Poem

White factories lancing sky
As the city grew near
Were symbols of changed state,

Pulse and strength of steel arms
Seemed hammering out new world
Not by you informed. The road

Led through the large morning
From that landscape, witness
Of Love's strange life, hard dying.

Absent, yet in loud street
You were, and in café,
And but wore her and her.

The cheating eyes, blood's tumult,
Wrote you more sure than those
Of senses' no and yes,

Whom place and minutes kill.
And when I thought you changed,
As hill and leaf for stone,

I thought out you who stand
On the inward side of sense –
Leaf, stone, are of your substance
And these ghosts whom I see.

[*Oxford Poetry* (1931), p. 38]

128

My pulling on of shoes
My opening of doors
Speaking – the hundred acts
That serve my hourly use

Are then not disparate
Are nationals of one blood;
Closer, the raiding eyes
The thoughts around each gate

Are surely dyed the same;
In these, too, lover is,
And I, since I have loved you,
In everything I change
On the world must write your name.

That for sense enough keen
Within a street I must
From the rest show different;
And though I walk still here
I breathe, from what I had been,
Your love's whole air distant.

[*Oxford Outlook*, vol. XII, no 57
(Feb. 1932), pp. 42–43]

For seeing whole I had been too near my friends:
When we drank or drove I came near to one,
Near to another in speaking of a woman:
What could I hold back, using their blood, their brain?

In part only I saw them. Then in the train
I crossed fields that had never known their fire;
An evening country turning, hedges and trees
Not leaved with their words and laughter, as those were.

The brow of Summer matched against their quickness
Made them seem far and overshadowed them.
They must spill apart and change whom I thought firm;
I saw them draw like green things to their time.

[*Oxford Poetry* (1932), p. 46]

APPENDIX B

TWO STATEMENTS ON POETRY

1. *Cairo 1942*

Folk poetry, both ancient and modern, shows a remarkable callousness (e.g. 'Och Johnny I hardly knew you . . .' and 'A handsome young airman lay dying . . .'). And J. Synge, a writer who was consciously basing his art on the life of the common people, said that poetry must become 'brutal'.

That is to say that more sophisticated poetry, if it is to have any force, has also to be rooted in the uncivilized layers of the mind, where what is ugly and what is beautiful can both be contemplated and do not exclude each other.

Nowadays, through living in a more urban and controlled society, a poet starts off with a tenderer heart and a weaker stomach than, let us say, an Elizabethan. To write good poetry he has to brutalize himself back out of his upbringing. His dangers are that, faced with injustice, violence and squalor, he may either get numb, frigid, over-intellectual, or soft, sentimental.

The capacity for pity and the capacity for scientific detachment may both be valuable to him in the rest of his life but they are dangerous to him as a poet. Pity and disgust and the scientific attitude are all attitudes of separation, not of joining. (Though pity or disgust might provide the necessary impulse to begin writing.) True poetry is a dance in which you take part and enjoy yourself.

This is the real meaning of the old definition of poetry as giving 'pleasure' (where we are inclined to say 'truth'). This, too, is what Yeats meant when he said, 'passive suffering is not a proper subject for poetry', and when he said, 'The Muses are women and love the embraces of the 'warty' (sexy) boys'.

B.S.

['*Ideas about Poems III,*' *Personal Landscape*, vol. I, part 4 (1942), p. 2]

2. *Vienna, 1963*

Recently I have been discovering again how limited the poet's control is of what he writes and when. At least it is for me. For instance you have had for some time a poem which you very much want to write, and you even have some 'given' lines or phrases towards it, an idea perhaps from these about the form it is likely to take, and a reasonable confidence that it is a real poem and not a phony one. And in spite of all this, what happens? You write instead another poem which swept you off your heels, love at sight, last Tuesday. It amounts to a breach of promise.

The breach of promise may be committed several times again, and at the expense of the same poem. A likely reason is the 'breeding' or 'chain' quality of poems. The excitement of the actual writing of a poem can illuminate for me a different bit of experience, and I am confronted with the compelling demand of another poem which wants to be written, and which would probably not otherwise have 'got through' to me.

I learnt long ago from the Greek poet, George Seferis, to think of poems as sometimes waiting around to be written, perhaps in certain parts of a town, until a poet comes along. But then, of course, he must be alert enough to recognise them. And what freaks of accident – or is it more than that – take him to the place where the poem is? And when he has written it, how contrary to what might have been anticipated, and to the writer's current preoccupations or views, the final result may be!

[from 'Bernard Spencer Writes . . .', *Poetry Book Society Bulletin*, no. 37 (June 1963)]

NOTES

For all poems published in *Aegean Islands* (1946) and *With Luck Lasting* (1963), together with 'Poems from Vienna,' from *Collected Poems* (1965), these notes provide, in order, the following information where available: existing worksheet, manuscript, typescript, or galley sources, with a brief description of any significant variations from the published text; first printed appearance, where applicable, in a periodical, anthology, or annual; and, finally, contextual details of particular interest. For uncollected poems the periodical publication provides the text, and with unpublished work, the first item cited is the source.

Principal Sources Cited

BOOKS BY BERNARD SPENCER

Aegean Islands and Other Poems (London: Editions Poetry,   AI
   (Nicholson and Watson, 1946)

The Twist in the Plotting (Reading: University of Reading School of   TP
   Art, 1960)

With Luck Lasting (London: Hodder & Stoughton, 1963)   WLL

Collected Poems (London: Alan Ross, 1965)   CP

[*Note*: The American editions of *Aegean Islands* (New York: Doubleday, 1948)
   and *With Luck Lasting* (Chester Springs, Penn.: Dufour Editions, 1965)
   duplicate the English texts.]

OTHER PRINTED SOURCES

The Year's Poetry and *Personal Landscape: An Anthology of Exile* are cited in full. Periodicals are also cited fully, with the place of publication when other than London, except for *Personal Landscape* (Cairo) and *Citadel* (Cairo), cited by title only.

Notes

UNPUBLISHED MATERIAL

(i) Libraries

The Library, University of Reading
  Manuscript and typescript sources   Reading MS. and TS.
  Fletcher correspondence   Reading Papers

Humanities Research Center, University of
Texas at Austin
  Six carbon typescripts and one galley   HRC TS.
  Lehmann correspondence   HRC Papers

The Poetry/Rare Books Collection of the
University Libraries, State University of New
York at Buffalo
  One typescript and one galley   Buffalo TS.

The Seferis Collection, Gennadius Library,
American School of Classical Studies, Athens
  Thirteen typescripts   Gennadius TS.

BBC Script Library
  'Poems by Bernard Spencer,' pre-recorded
  for Third Programme, July 30, 1959   BBC

(ii) In private hands
Worksheets, manuscripts, and typescripts in
possession of Mrs Anne Humphreys   Humphreys MS. and T'
Additional material in Mrs Humphreys'
possession   AH Papers

Other manuscripts in the possession of Roger
Bowen, John Fitzgibbon, Melanie Isaacs, and
Clover Pertinez cited by owner's surname
only. Letters received by Mrs Pertinez cited by
name and date.

Aegean Islands and Other Poems

POEMS BEFORE 1940

Page

1   *Allotments: April*
    New Verse, no. 21 (June-July 1936), pp. 4–5.

3   *A Hand*
    New Verse, no. 17 (Oct.–Nov. 1935), p. 4.

4   *Plains as Large as Europe*
    New Verse, no. 13 (Feb. 1935), p. 4. I have restored 'certainty,'; 1. 12;
    AI has 'certainly'

5   *There was no Instruction Given*
    New Verse, no. 15 (June 1935), p. 2.

Notes

6 *Houses are Uniformed*
New Verse, no. 17 (Oct.–Nov. 1935), p. 5, as 'Poem.'

8 *Evasions*
New Verse no. 17 (Oct.–Nov. 1935), p. 4.

9 *Portrait of a Woman and Others*
New Verse, no. 13 (Feb. 1935), pp. 4–5.

10 *A Cold Night*
New Verse, no. 24 (Feb.–Mar. 1937), pp. 8–9.

11 *Part of Plenty*
New Verse, no. 24 (Feb.–Mar. 1937), pp. 10–11. The subject is Nora, his first wife.

12 *Cage*
Year's Poetry, ed. D. K. Roberts & Geoffrey Grigson (London: Lane-Bodley Head, 1937), p. 105.

13 *Ill*
New Verse, no. 24 (Feb.–Mar. 1937), p. 10.

14 *A Thousand Killed*
New Verse, no. 20 (April–May 1936), p. 11.

15 *Suburb Factories*
New Verse, no. 20 (April–May 1936), p. 10, incl. between the 4th and 5th stanzas of the version in *AI* and *CP*:

> From the diamonded parks I would wish to delight
> At shapes that attack and are new:
> But it's hard,
> Knowing only for certain; power is here surrendered
> And it changes to the hands of the few.

16 *Waiting*
New Verse, no. 29 (March 1938), p. 12.

17 *How Must we Live?*
'Poetry Supplement,' The Listener (12 July 1933), facing p. 76.

18 *My Sister*
New Verse, no. 13 (Feb. 1935), p. 5 untitled. Spencer's father, Sir Charles Gordon Spencer, died at his home, Tarwood House, South Leigh, Oxfordshire, in November, 1934; Cynthia Peppercorn, bearing a child, was reunited with her brothers, Bernard and John, at the family home.

POEMS 1940 TO 1942

19 *Aegean Islands 1940–41*
Gennadius TS.; publ. Personal Landscape, no. 1 (Jan. 1942), p. 4.

20 *Greek Excavations*
Gennadius TS., signed; publ. Personal Landscape, no. 1 (Jan. 1942), p. 5, Citadel (Feb. 1942), p. 7. For *AI* Spencer transposes '– And I

suddenly discover this discovered town' from the last line of st. 1 to the first of st. 2.

21 *Salonika June 1940*
Gennadius TS., signed.

22 *Delos*
Gennadius TS., with first 9 lines trans. into Greek by Seferis; publ. *Personal Landscape*, no. 1 (Jan. 1942), p. 6. CP omits 2nd 'violence,' l. 17. 'One day I went to Delos, that island across the water from Mykonos where in ancient times there was a famous oracle. The city has been largely excavated and it is a strange experience to walk in the streets which died nearly 2000 years ago, and in the market, the harbour district and the residential area, where you can still see the fine mosaic floors laid down in the houses by the rich merchants.' 'The Wind-blown Island of Mykonos,' *The Listener* (5 Sept. 1946), pp. 307–8. The same article suggests a context for 'Peasant Festival.'

23 *Base Town*
Gennadius TS.; Publ. *Personal Landscape*, no. 2 (March 1942), p. 15.

24 *Death of an Airman*
Gennadius TS.; publ. *Citadel* (April 1942), p. 23.

25 *Letters*
Gennadius TS.; publ. *Personal Landscape*, no. 3 (June 1942), p. 11 with l. 9, 'Now public truths are scarce as sovereigns.'

27 *Egyptian Delta*
Gennadius TS., with fifth line trans. into Greek by Seferis.

28 *Acre*
Personal Landscape, vol. I, part 4 (1942), p. 5; Spencer spent 2 week summer leave in Palestine in 1942 and 1943.

29 *Frontier*
Gennadius TS.; publ. *Personal Landscape*, Vol. I, part 4 (1942), p. 4

30 *Cairo Restaurant*
Gennadius TS.

31 *The Ship*
Personal Landscape, Vol. 2, part 2 (1944), p. 7. The setting wa Nahariah, Palestine.

32 *Behaviour of Money*
Personal Landscape, vol. 2, pt. 1 (1943), p. 15–16.

33 *Yachts on the Nile*
Publ. *Personal Landscape: An Anthology of Exile* (London: Editior Poetry, 1945), p. 64.

35 *The Building of the House*
Personal Landscape, vol. 2, pt. 2 (1944), p. 8. Variants incl. ll. 5–ŝ 'features from it, and eyes to see: such fancies/and all the tumble an ballet of building gear,' l. 9, 'were portrait-maker's touches, cool feeling,' and l. 21, 'which never touched us to the bone?'

37 *Egyptian Dancer at Shubra*
    Personal Landscape, vol. 2, pt. 3 (1944), p. 6, as 'Dancer at Shubra.'

38 *Passed On*
    Personal Landscape, vol. 2, part 1 (1943), p. 16, as 'Passed Over.'
    Variants incl. 11. 4–5, 'in desks and scrapbooks, what he used to call/
    visitors and uncles,' and 1. 13, 'even rough horseplay, crashing a table
    about.'

39 *In an Auction Room*
    Personal Landscape, vol. 2, part 4 (1945), p. 12.

40 *Sarcophagi*
    Gennadius TS.; publ. *Personal Landscape*, vol. I, part 4 (1942), p. 3.
    CP combines st. 3 and 4.

With Luck Lasting

41 *The Beginning*
    Reading TS.

42 *Delicate Grasses*
    Reading TS., 11. 9–10, 'slow as the seconds wear/or dial needles prowl,'
    with autograph revision. Publ. *New Statesman* (May 14, 1960), p. 719,
    as 'Feathery Grasses,' and in *TP*. 'After crossing the plain [of Anatolia]
    we drove over the mountains to look at the remains of some ancient
    Greek towns on the south coast of Turkey. These towns, although
    overgrown with grass and weeds, often have recognizable remains of
    temples and theatres standing, with their semi-circular tiers of stone
    seats. So much emptiness and all those ruins put me in a state of
    melancholy excitement. I was half-attracted by it and half afraid . . .
    What is the trap? What was I afraid of? Later, at his request, I read the
    poem out to John Betjeman, and he cried out "Oh! Eternity!" That is as
    good an answer as any.' (Madrid University lecture, March 1962, AH
    Papers.)

43 *Notes by a Foreigner*
    Reading MS., signed, as 'The Foreigner'; variants incl. 11. 1–2, 'Deep
    in their kind of eyes/you imagine gleams some truth about this town.'
    Reading TS., as 'Notes by a Foreigner.' Publ. *London Magazine* (Dec.
    1955), pp. 28–29.

44 *From my Window*
    Reading TS., 1. 1, 'Now that.'

45 *Mediterranean Suburbs*
    Reading MS., 'As it Happens'; variants incl. 11. 12–17, 'a few small
    boys have left their games to romp/around the scarecrow player. Streets
    and evening/family, music, beggar; all these are/connected or not,
    would you say good or not,/are, as it happens, now and in Castilla/under
    the eternities of that first-starred sky.' Humphreys TS., 'As it Happens';
    Reading MS., autograph revisions 11. 12–17, and Reading TS., as

'Madrid Suburbs,' revisions complete. Reading TS. as 'Mediterranean Suburbs'.

46   *Fluted Armour*
Reading MS., l. 1, 'Because of the splintering of every day,' (deleted); further autograph revisions. Reading TS., l. 6, 'particular things' to 'a confusion of particulars.' Publ. *London Magazine* (August 1955), p. 33.

47   *Out of Sleep*
Reading TS.; Publ. *Poetry (London)*, no.11 (Sept.–Oct. 1947), pp. 12–13.

48   *A Spring Wind*
Gennadius TS., with 'Seferis' underlined in red; l. 1 has 'slam to' and l. 16, 'its tide.' Reading TS., with 'slam to' deleted and autograph revision. Publ. *The Windmill* vol. I, no. 1 (1946), p. 55.

49   *On a Carved Axle-Piece from a Sicilian Cart*
Reading TS., l. 22, 'the who and what and why of God and us' (deleted), with autograph revision. *Penguin New Writing*, 32 (1947), pp. 78–9.

50   *The Boats*
Reading TS.; publ. *Penguin New Writing* 37 (1949), p. 82.

51   *At Courmayeur*
Reading TS., l. 14, 'to draw more closely,' and l. 17, 'is hard and real as rocks' (deleted), with autograph revisions. Publ. *Penguin New Writing* 37 (1949), p. 81. In memory of Nora; see also G. S. Fraser's 'The Absence of the Dead,' *The Traveller has Regrets* (London: Editions Poetry, 1948), pp. 2–3.

52   *In a Foreign Hospital*
Reading TS.; Buffalo TS. and galley, signed, with l. 16 'England is somewhere far enough to my right;' publ. *Poetry Review*, XL, no. 3 (June-July 1949), p. 177. Spencer entered the Beau-Soleil Clinic, Leysin, Switzerland, Sept. 2nd, 1948 for thoracotomy. 'There is no special connection between Parts I and II of "In a Foreign Hospital." They might easily appear separately. It's just that the title seemed to suit both.' (Letter to John Lehmann, Nov. 18, 1948, HRC Papers) Only one 'part' appears to have been published, and to have survived.

53   *Regent's Park Terrace*
Reading TS.; *Poetry (London)* (Nov.–Dec. 1947), p. 23.

54   *Letter Home*
Reading worksheet with autograph revisions, and TS. with l. 9, 'names of cargoes and iron harbours' (deleted) and autograph revision. Reading Papers, letter to Ian Fletcher, Nov. 5, 1954, 'a little reminder of Cairo (Zamalek).'

55   *Morning in Madrid*
Reading TS., as 'Early Morning Madrid.'

56 *The Café with the Blue Shrine*
Reading MS., as 'Flamenco' with autograph revisions; variants incl. 11.
18–20, 'doubtless approved a different harmony/of world and when and
home we never came/within years or vineyards of; who watched the
swaggerers stand.' Reading TS., 'The Café with the Blue Shrine,' 1. 18,
'heard in his bones that song' (deleted), with autograph revision. Publ.
London Magazine (August 1955), p. 32.

57 *Castanets*
Reading MS., with variants incl. 11. 9–12, 'I watch her body kindle and
glow/and a knife in her glance/ and wonder at the icy/shiver of pleasure
now;' Reading TS. Publ. *London Magazine* (Dec. 1955), p. 29.

58 *In Athens*
Reading MSS.; one MS., initialled, ends:
>An alteration of pulse,
>and a word your body is trying to make you hear
>is all you are left with on a city corner,
>as she goes past, hair flapped across her cheek,
>so near where they talked well on love
>two civilizations ago, and found
>splendid and jeering images: 'the Blind,'
>'the Wounder,' 'the Unknowable,'
>A word your body is trying to make you . . .?
>– the last wry joke: the split
>apple that famishes for its perfect half.

Reading MS., as publ., marked 'new version', and TS.; Isaacs MS.,
signed; Bowen MS., initialled, with last three lines of above stanza
deleted. Publ. *New Statesman* (6 April 1957), p. 436.

59 *The Rendezvous*
Reading worksheets and initialled MS.; 1. 11; 'since smashed windows,
cars on fire;' Reading TS. Publ. *London Magazine* (April 1957), p. 45.

60 *The Lottery Sellers*
Isaacs MS., with variants incl. 11. 1–2, 'Under a pewter sky/–passers are
muffled and the snow-wind races;' Reading TS., 1. 15, 'on a hell-cold
corner' (deleted), with autograph revision. Publ. *London Magazine*
(April 1957), p. 46.

61 *Train to Work*
Reading TS.

62 *At 'The Angler'*
Reading MS., initialled, with st. 4:
>A little of the ideal suffices lovers:
>for instance, with the end of storm
>how swans curved near as if to bring good omen
>to us – whom love's worst love had wrung
>too frequently – and in their trance of calm
>possessed like many lamps the water where they hung.

Bowen MS. with further revisions in this stanza, incl. 1. 24, 'blinded the water where they hung.' Reading TS., with autograph revision of st. 4. Publ. *New Statesman* (16 Feb. 1957), p. 208.

63 *The Administrator*
Reading TS., 1. 10, 'impulsive' to 'passionate,' an autograph revision, and 1. 18, rep. 'but cold' added. *London Magazine* (July 1960), p. 67; 1. 18, second 'But cold, ' omitted.

64 *Night-time: Starting to Write*
Reading MS., with alternate title, 'Writing at Night.' Other variants include 1. 7, 'Idly I note these sounds,' and 1. 11, ' – must play a loved-loathed role; ' Reading TS.

65 *Sud-Express*
Reading MS. and TS., signed.

66 *Boat Poem*
Reading worksheets; HRC carbon TS. Publ. *London Magazine* (Feb . 1962), pp. 17–19; 1. 28 omitted. The setting is Ibiza.

68 *Table-Tennis*
HRC carbon TS. Publ. *London Magazine* (June 1962), p. 5.

69 *The Leopards*
HRC carbon TS. Publ. *London Magazine* (June 1962), pp. 5–6.

70 *A Sunday*
Reading MS., as 'Plaza de Toros' (deleted); 1. 9, 'laughter like gravel falling;' HRC carbon TS. Publ. *London Magazine* (June 1962), p. 6. The setting is Chinchon, near Madrid.

71 *Cripples*
Reading worksheets and MSS.; as 'Crutches' (deleted). Variants include 1. 9, 'heave acres of vineyards towards months of sun.' HRC carbon TS. Publ. *London Magazine* (June 1962), pp. 6–7.

72 *Watchers*
Reading worksheet and MS.; variant titles, 'High Trapeze' and 'The Sleepers.' Other variants include 11. 10–11, 'These are like faces drained in sleep. There stays/no thought in them for field or hearth or children.' HRC carbon TS. as 'Watchers'. Publ. *London Magazine* (June 1962), p. 7.

73 *The Wedding Pictures*
Reading worksheet and MSS., minor revisions. Publ. *London Magazine* (Jan. 1963), pp. 8–9.

74 *By a Breakwater*
Reading worksheet and MSS.; variant title, 'At Dover.' Final line deleted: 'After ten years I feel myself walking and turning to look again down the wind.' Publ. *London Magazine* (Jan. 1963), pp. 7–8.

75 *Lop-sided*
Reading worksheet, as 'Meteorology,' with variants incl. 1. 9, 'We had noticed no adequate preliminaries.'

76 *Donkey*
    London Magazine (Nov. 1960), p. 30.

77 *Full Moon*
    Reading worksheet; TS., with minor revisions. 'The poem about the
    moon was written in Athens during my time there (1955–56) . . . The
    full moon – and the cry of mating cats – play a great part in my
    memories of the town' (letter to Pertinez, Aug. 12, 1963), Publ. *London
    Magazine* (April 1957), p. 46.

78 *The Agents*
    Reading MS., heavily revised, as 'Her Agents.' Variants incl. 1. 18:
    'such long years of frost-fire.' Publ. *London Magazine* (Nov. 1960), p.
    31.

79 *Chestnuts*
    London Magazine (Nov. 1960), p. 31. Reading Papers, letter to
    Fletcher, 2 Feb. 1960, 'I got the idea when I was staying in Bucking-
    hamshire last September–October.' Spencer's brother, John Spencer-
    Bernard, was bequeathed Nether Winchendon House and the estate,
    near Aylesbury, in 1954.

80 *Blue Arm*
    Reading worksheet; Reading and Pertinez MSS., initialled, with var-
    iants incl. 1. 6, 'sunhaze,' 1.7, 'Perhaps it is all an answer,' 1. 12, 'the
    blue arm fumbles a window.' Publ. *London Magazine* (Nov. 1960), p.
    32. [WLL and CP have 'peelings' in 1. 1; I have restored 'peeling' from
    Pertinez and *London Magazine* versions]. Reading Papers, letter to
    Fletcher, ref. *TP*, 'If you would consider putting in the poem "Blue
    Arm" of which I enclose a copy (it is new) and calling the collection by
    that title. It would mean knocking out the poem "Night Time: Starting
    to Write," which is rather on the same theme.'

81 *Near Aranjuez*
    Reading TS.; 1. 13 has, 'the Romans found' (deleted), with autograph
    revision. Publ. *London Magazine* (August 1955), p. 33, with orig. TS.
    version.

82 *On the Road*
    Reading TS. Publ. *Penguin New Writing*, no. 32 (1947), p. 79. '[it] has
    a setting in France, at a place along the River Loire. The theme is the
    possibility of entirely perfect and happy episodes in life, although the
    title implies that they do not usually last very long.' (BBC)

Collected Poems

POEMS FROM VIENNA

83 *The Empire Clock*
    Reading TS., with autograph revisions and variants, incl. 1. 2, 'muffled
    gnashing,' and 1. 5, 'long voiceless.' Publ. *London Magazine* (Sept.
    1963), p. 4.

84 *On the 'Sievering' Tram*
Pertinez MS., initialled. Publ. *London Magazine* (Sept. 1963), pp. 4–5.

85 *The Invaders*
London Magazine (Sept. 1963), pp. 5–6.

86 *A Number*
Humphreys MS., with variants incl. 1. 17, 'I thought you were calling out the stitches that you are always counting.' Final line in published version added after birth of Piers Spencer. Publ. *London Magazine* (Sept. 1963), p. 6.

87 *Properties of Snow*
London Magazine (Sept. 1963), pp. 6–7.

88 *Clemente*
Humphreys MS. and worksheet; Bowen MS. and Humphreys TS. end:
> Addressed by a girl in Madrid to winter-haunted Vienna:
> 'item . . . item . . . item . . . Clemente died . . . item.'

> With what was his smile, once,
> with what he would boast of,
> Clemente who wangled you the cruel drinks.

HRC galley. Publ. *London Magazine* (Dec. 1963), p. 13.

89 *You*
London Magazine (Jan. 1964), p. 47.

90 *Dr Karl Lueger*
London Magazine (Jan. 1964), p. 48.

91 *To Piers Spencer*
London Magazine (Jan. 1964), pp. 48–49.

92 *Traffic in April*
London Magazine (Jan. 1964), p. 49.

Poems previously uncollected and unpublished

93 'Most things having a market price'
New Verse (June 1935), p. 2.

94 'I Jack, walking on the hill's shoulder'
New Verse (June 1935), pp. 2–3.

95 *The Runner*
New Verse (June 1935), p. 3.

96 *Winter Landscape*
Spectator (April 24, 1936), p. 751. Spencer's brief Oxford memoir, 'Talking of Barry, ' *Esfam* (Cairo), May 1944, pp. 2–4, suggests the occasion and the place – Port Meadow.

97 *The House*
New Verse (April–May 1936), p. 11.

Notes

98 *Going to the Country*
    New Verse (Feb.–Mar. 1937), pp. 9–10.

99 *Picked Clean from the World*
    New Verse (Jan. 1938), p. 4.

100 *They Tell a Lie*
    Gennadius TS., attached to 'Death of an Airman.' First two stanzas
    inscribed inside cover of Seferis's copy of *Aegean Islands*, dated
    Groppi's, Cairo, June 1941. Cited in Seferis's diary, *Days: 1st January,
    1941 to 31st December 1944* (Athens: Icarus, 1977), pp. 106–7, where
    he recalls meeting Spencer at Groppi's on 27th June and being shown
    this recently completed poem. Also cited in Seferis's essay, 'The Greek
    Poems of Lawrence Durrell,' *Labrys* (July 1979), pp. 91–92, trans.
    Anthony Tyrrell.

101 *In Memoriam*
    Reading TS.; incl. in autograph list of 22 poems, some published, some
    in MS., others untraced; those publ. date from 1946 to 1955.

102 *The Top-Storey Room*
    The Windmill, vol. II, no. 1 (1946), p. 54.

103–7 Montale Translations
    Reading MS.; pencilled drafts, with revisions, inserted in Spencer's copy
    of *Ossi di Seppia* (Torino: Giulio Einaudi, 1942). 'I limoni,' from
    'Movimenti'; 'Non chierdici la parola,' 'Merrigiare pallido e assorto,'
    and 'Portami il girasole,' from 'Ossi di Seppia.' Probably trans. Palermo
    or Turin, Sept. 1946 to August 1948.

108 *Pino*
    Poetry (London), no. 15 (May 1949), p. 5; Reading TS. has autograph
    insert between l. 16 and 17, 'the road of foreboding and of dreadful
    hope.'

109 *Casa de P_____.*
    Pertinez MS. and Fitzgibbon carbon TS.; privately circulated poem,
    Madrid c. 1950.

110 *The Clock*
    Reading TS; Humphreys MS with minor variants. Listed with 'In
    Memoriam;' Madrid setting.

111 *For Signorina Brunella Mori*
    Reading TS.; listed with 'In Memoriam,' and 'The Clock.'

112 *A Ward*
    Reading TS; Reading MS., as 'A Departure,' with minor variants, and,
    with worksheet, as 'The Grapes,' with substantial differences, incl. st. 3:

    > She might have found one, she did as much, that nurse
    > who ran back, while we stared, and fetched from the curtains
    > (or from remotest hills) a swinging cluster of
    > foggy-blue grapes, and carried them through a silence . . .

    Spencer admitted to St. George's Hospital, Brompton Road, S.W.1,
    Aug. 1959.

113 *Black Cat*
Reading MS., initialled; deletion foll. 1. 16, 'kicking up gravel, in a remembering mood (vein). ' Publ. *London Magazine* (Dec. 1979–Jan. 1980), p. 102.

114 *Castille*
Humphreys TS; Reading MS., signed, and worksheet with variants incl. final stanza:
> If I am gentle I shall come to know
> Contradiction bitterer than ours
> The gilded Christs and a landscape shaped like pain
> The dust and the oxen's fast and the bones and crowns
> and flowers.

115 *This Day*
Reading MS.; Humphreys MS., heavily deleted, and worksheet, suggest a poem of greater length. Variants substantial, incl. first st.: '"I love you" her first words were/ "I love you" first; and then the rendezvous,/the silly phone, her diffident low voice/goodbyes, endearments, were the ones I knew.'

116 *Witness*
Reading TS., dated Dec. 1962; Reading MS. with minor variants.

117 *Written on a Cigarette Packet*
Publ. *London Magazine* (Jan. 1963), p. 7; Humphreys TS. and 'worksheet', notes composed on a packet of Senior Service.

118 *From the Military Academy*
Reading TS.; Reading MS. with autograph revisions. 'The "bugles" poem in the new lot is another one with reference to Breton de los Herreros' (Letter to Pertinez, Jan. 1963). Spencer lived on this Madrid street for a time during his second posting, Sept. 1958 to July 1962.

119 *The Train Window*
Reading TS.; Humphreys worksheet and MS., with autograph revisions. Publ. *London Magazine* (Dec. 1979–Jan. 1980), pp. 101–102.

Unpublished Poems: A bibliographical note

The Reading archives contain the following items not printed here:
'The girl in the black mantilla with the ink-splash eyes' (Unfinished, untitled MS. of 11 lines)
'Look at my suit' (10 line fragment)
Untitled contribution, of 12 lines, to *Epitalamia*, by various hands for the nuptials of George Sutherland Fraser and Eileen Lucy Andrew, London, printed by Wyndham Printers Limited for Tambimuttu, 1946.
'For madmen, darkness whip and chain' (untitled fragment of 20 lines, rhyming couplets; Cairo setting suggested)
'Rocks like a Durer landscape, torn and hacked' (untitled, 40 lines, extensively revised)

Notes

Appendix A: Oxford Poems

Those poems not included in my selection, listed chronologically, are:

'Collection', *Oxford Outlook*, vol. X, no. 50 (Nov. 1929), p. 362.

'Above, the fingers of the tree,' *Oxford Poetry* (1930), p. 36.

'Departure,' *Oxford Poetry* (1930), p. 37.

'The hills begin their march again; Pauline,' *Oxford Poetry* (1930), p. 37.

'Those Near and Dead,' *Oxford Poetry* (1930), p. 38.

'Her Hands waking on her lap,' *Oxford Outlook*, vol. XII, no. 57 (Feb. 1932), p. 43, and *Oxford Poetry*, (1932), p. 45.

'Who sees the rain fall into the Spring land,' *Oxford Outlook*, vol. XII, no. 58 (May 1932), p. 132.

'Such Height of Corn,' *Oxford Poetry* (1932), p. 47.

Appendix B: Two Statements on Poetry

1. There are echoes here of an earlier estimation of Auden: 'Auden doesn't go soft and sermonize. Because our pity is appealed to so much, an emotion you can't live with for long at a stretch, sermonizing is a particular fault of contemporary poets. He succeeds in brutalizing his thought and language to the level from which important poetry proceeds.' *New Verse*, Auden Double Number (Nov. 1937) , p. 27.

2. The reader may also wish to consult Spencer's response to a questionnaire on modern poetry and the modern poet, 'Context,' *London Magazine* (Feb. 1962), pp. 41–42. The full text of his interview with Peter Orr – *The Poet Speaks* (London: Routledge & Kegan Paul. 1966), pp. 233–237 – remains invaluable.

INDEX OF FIRST LINES

147